# Art and Swadeshi

# Art and Swadeshi

Ananda K. Coomaraswamy

ISBN: 978-93-5128-913-5(HB)

First Published in 1912
Indian Reprint in 2017

*Published by*

Kalpaz Publications
C-30, Satyawati Nagar,
Delhi – 110052
E-mail: kalpaz@hotmail.com
Website: kalpazpublications.com
Ph.: +91-9212142040

**Cataloging in Publication Data—DK**
Courtesy: D.K. Agencies (P) Ltd. <docinfo@dkagencies.com>

**Coomaraswamy, Ananda K. (Ananda Kentish),** 1877-1947., **author.**
Art and swadeshi / Ananda K. Coomaraswamy.
pages cm
Reprint. Originally published: Madras : Ganesh & Co., [1912].
Includes index.
ISBN 9789351289135 (HB)

1. Arts, Indic. I. Title.

NX576.A1C66 2017 DDC 700.954 23

# Contents

*List of Illustrations* vi

1. Art and Swadeshi 1
2. Swadeshi, True and False 7
3. Domestic Handicraft and Culture 19
4. The International Congress of Applied Chemistry 1901: and Aniline Dyes 30
5. The Function of Schools of Art in India: A Reply to Mr. Cecil Burns 36
6. On the Study of Indian Art 46
7. Facial Expression in Indian Sculpture 56
8. On Mughal and Rajput Painting 63
9. Night Effects in Indian Pictures 81
10. Song-words of a Panjabi Singer 88
11. Poems of Rabindranath Tagore 102
12. The Modern School of Indian Painting 116
13. Education in Ceylon 128

*Index* 140

# List of Illustrations


I. Weavers in the Streets, Tanjore 20

II. Buddha, Ceylon 57

III. Siva, Tanjore 59

IV. Sundaramurti Swami, Ceylon 61

V. Yogis: Illustration to Persian translation of the Yoga Vashishta 66

VI. The Dying Man: Mughal Miniature in the Bodleian, Oxford 71

VII. Rajput drawing from Jaipur, Bodleian, Oxford 73

VIII. Ragini Tori: Rajput picture from Jaipur 77

IX. The Divine Cowherd: Rajput picture from Kangra 78

X. Riding at Night (Collection of Mr. C.H. Read) 82

XI. Golden Rain 84

XII. Uma Worshipping Siva 85

XIII. The Bride 86

XIV. Devadasi (by A.N. Tagore) 117

XV. Rama and the Magic Deer (by A.N. Tagore) 119

XVI. Kaikeyi (by Nand Lal Bose) 121

XVII. The Goddess of Earth offering Sandals to Rama (by Venkata Appa) 123

XVIII. Krishna and Yasoda (by Asit Kumar Haldar) 125

# 1

# Art and Swadeshi*

If you go into one of those shops frequented by tourists in Indian towns, you will find amongst the flimsy wood carving and shallow brass work, the cheap enamels and the overloaded embroideries which are outward manifestations of the degradation of Indian craftsmanship, a few examples of real old Indian manufactures. These things, which used to be common in every market and were at once the wealth of the Indian people and the basis of their export trade for the last three thousand years, are now rare and difficult to obtain; they are called *purani chiz*, 'old things'. They are bought by American connoisseurs and German collectors for museums, for the education of Europe in design and for the benefit of the European manufacturer, for whom, too, they are reproduced in such papers as the *Journal of Indian Art*, and lectured on in Technical Schools and Schools of Art. For while the creative power of the craftsman has been long destroyed by commercialism in the West, it remained alive with us till yesterday, and even today some part of it survives.

Indian design is an inexhaustible treasure-house of fine invention. But have you ever reflected that all this invention belongs to the past—that modern India, Anglicised India, has produced no beauty and romance, but has gone far to destroy the beauty and romance which are our heritage from the past? Go into a Swadeshi shop—you will not find the evidences of

*Reprinted from the *Central Hindu College Magazine*. This essay has also appeared in the *Message of the East* which will not be reprinted in its present form.

Indian invention, the wealth of beauty which the Indian craftsman used to lavish on the simplest articles of daily use, the filmy muslins or the flower-woven silks with which we used to worship the beauty of Indian women, the brazen vessels from which we ate and drank, the carpets on which we trod with bare feet or the pictures that revealed to us the love of Radha, or the soul of the eternal snows. You will not find these things, but you will find every kind of imitation of the productions of European commerce, differing only from their unlovely prototypes in their slightly higher price and slightly inferior quality. You will find dingy grey 'shirtings'; other materials dyed with aniline dyes of the loudest and least permanent; travelling trunks that are painted every colour of the rainbow, and if carefully used may hold together for half a year; boot polish, marking ink, soaps and fountain pens—anything and everything but beauty. It is the outward sign of the merely material ideal of prosperity which is too exclusively striven for by our economists and politicians. I shall show presently how even such an aim defeats itself, but in the meanwhile let us take another view.

You are familiar with the thought that the highest ideal of nationality is service. Have you ever thought that India, politically and economically free, but subdued by Europe in her inmost soul is scarcely an ideal to be dreamt of, or to live, or die, for? "India, vulgarised by modern education, and by the ideals of modern commercialism, will never compensate humanity for India with its knowledge of beauty." Have you ever realised that there are European artists who believe that when a new inspiration comes into European art it will come again from the East? Do you realise that when India was a great political power in Asia, when she colonised Java and inspired China, this also was the period of her greatest achievement in art? Has it never occurred to you that it is as much your duty to make your lives and your environment beautiful as to make them moral, in fact that without beauty there can be no true morality, without morality no true beauty? Look round about you at the vulgarisation of modern India—our prostitution of art to the tourist trade—our use of kerosene tins for water jars, and galvanised zinc for tiles—our caricature of European dress—our homes furnished and ornamented in the style proverbial of seaside lodging houses, with cut glass chandeliers and China dogs and artificial flowers—our devotion to the harmonium and the gramophone—these things are the outward and damning proof of "some mighty evil in our souls".

Try to believe that this callousness of ours, this loss of the fine taste that belonged to classic and mediaeval culture is a sign of weakness, not of strength. Try to believe in the regeneration of India through art, and not by politics and economics alone. A purely material idea will never give to us the lacking strength to build up a great enduring nation. For that we need ideals and dreams, impossible and visionary, the food of martyrs and of artists.

You see, this loss of beauty in our lives is a proof that we do not love India; for India, above all nations, was beautiful once, and that was not long ago. It is the weakness of our national movement that we do not love India; we love suburban England, we love the comfortable bourgeois prosperity that is to be some day established when we have learned enough science and forgotten enough art to successfully compete with Europe in a commercial war conducted on its present lines. It is not thus that nations are made. And so, like Mr. Havell, I would say to you, "Leave off asking Government to revive your art and industries; all that is worth having you must and can do for yourselves; and when you have achieved all that you can do, no Government would refuse to grant you the political rights you desire, for the development of your artistic faculties will give back to India the creative force her people have lost. It will infuse into all your undertakings the practical sense and power of organisation which are now so often wanting."

And now for the practical side of the question, to show, i.e., that the ideal is (as always) the practical *par excellence.* The loss of artistic understanding more than anything else has ruined Indian industries and prevents the possibility of their revival. The neglect of Indian music has taken away the livelihood of the maker of musical instruments, with their hereditary and exquisite skill; has likewise destroyed the livelihood of Indian musicians; and fifteen lakhs worth of foreign instruments are annually imported from abroad! Observe that this is a double loss—material on the one hand, and spiritual on the other, for not only has the community lost wealth in the shape of things, but wealth in the shape of men, men who possessed the cunning and the skill to make them. Were India rich enough to spend a hundred lakhs per year on gramophones and harmoniums, this loss of men would still remain.

So too with the village weaver. Indian colouring and design have not been understood and loved: result, that the weaver's livelihood is gone, and he has to compete in agriculture, or in service in an already overcrowded field. Again, by concentration on the purely material side of the question, but not recognizing the superior workmanship of hand-made and individually designed materials, it has come about that instead of attempting to restore the village weaver and the handloom, we are willing to waste the vital forces of the nation in child-labour and long hours of work under mechanical and unhealthy conditions, transferred from Manchester to India. Remember that it can be said of England that "There is collected a population in our great towns which equals in amount the whole of those who lived in England and Wales six centuries ago; but whose condition is more destitute, whose homes are more squalid, whose means are more uncertain, whose prospects are more hopeless than those of the poorest serf of the middle ages and the meanest drudges of the mediaeval cities." Remember that one-tenth of the English people die in the work-house, the gaol or the lunatic asylum. Therefore learn not to waste the vital forces of the nation in a temporary political conflict, but understand that art will enable you to re-establish all your arts and industries on a surer basis, a basis which will bring well-being to the people themselves; for no lovely thing can be produced in conditions that are themselves unlovely.

Take one concrete case. "The Mirzapur carpets were at one time admired for their fast, bright colour, but are now identified with whatever is inferior in the name of dye or design. Aniline dyes and foreign models are responsible for the decline of a trade which gave fair promise of development not many years ago." Now observe that mere bad taste alone, the lack of artistic understanding, in such a case has destroyed the livelihood of the maker of dyes and the maker of carpets, and ruined even the possibility of an export trade.

The truth is that without artistic understanding, Indian manufacture cannot be effectively restored. It is suicidal to compete with Europe on a basis of cheapness. Competition should be upon a basis of quality.

At the same time the competition in cheapness alone is destructive of the very fibre of the Indian people: for "industry without art is brutality".

Swadeshi must be something more than a political weapon. It must be a religious-artistic ideal. I have heard nationalists exhort each other to sacrifice, in using Swadeshi goods. To think that it should need to be called a sacrifice! At least it should not, as now, be a sacrifice both in cost *and* quality. If we loved and understood Indian art we should know that even now the Indian craftsman could, if we would let him, build for us and clothe us in ways of beauty that could not be attained to in modern Europe for any expenditure of money at all. We would if we might, even today, live like the very gods but we lust after the fleshpots of Egypt, and deservedly our economy suffers.

Therefore I say to the well-to-do, that it is better to spend two hundred and fifty rupees on a Benares Sari, dyed with the country dyes, though two hundred would pay for it dyed in aniline, than to subscribe ten times that amount to some Swadeshi factory for making nibs or cloth and from which you expect a handsome dividend. And for the poor also in proportion to their ability remembering that "a poor man, by building the smallest temple, is no less meritorious than a wealthy man who builds the largest".*

Remember also that from the standpoint of national wealth, a few possessions that will endure, are better than many that will last only for a day. The builder whose work will last five centuries adds more to the national wealth than he whose work lasts only for fifty years. So, too, the weaver whose fair work is handed on from generation to generation does more for his country than a weaver whose work has soon to be cast aside. Civilisation consists not in multiplying the quantity of our desires, but in the refinement of their quality.

But let us not love art because it will bring to us prosperity; rather because it is a high function of our being, a door for thoughts to pass from the unseen to the seen, the source of those high dreams and the embodiment of that enduring vision that is to be the Indian nation; not less, but more strong and more beautiful than ever before, and the gracious giver of beauty to all the nations of the earth.

---

**Agni Purana,* ch. XXVIII.

# 2

## Swadeshi, True and False*

All those who have studied the Industrial Arts of India unite in recognizing and deploring their profound decay, and in very many cases, their practical extinction. Investigation invariably shows that goods that ought to be, and once were, common in the market, are now only to be seen in museums. One hundred, or even fifty years ago, it would have been possible to fill many museums worthily with the everyday handiwork of Indian artisans: now this would be only possible after years of patient collecting in remote districts. During the nineteenth century India has in fact, ceased to excel in those Industrial arts which provided the bulk of her exports, the main source of her wealth (after agriculture), and of the refined luxury of her homes during a period of time that must be counted in millenniums.

During this period—if we are to judge from the wreckage of her Industrial arts remaining to us—we must rank the civilisation of India indeed highly, for it could have been truly said that in her homes, whether of rich or poor, there could be found nothing that was not either useful or beautiful. In exchange for this world of beauty that was our birthright, the nineteenth century has made of our country a 'dumping-ground' for all the vulgar superfluities of European over-production; and all that the Swadeshi movement of the twentieth century has done is to provide us with many spurious imitations of these unlovely inutilities.

*Read at the Fifth Annual Industrial Conference, Allahabad, 1910.

It could hardly have been otherwise, for behind the Swadeshi movement there is no serious and consistent ideal. Its leaders have had but one thought before them—to save money. The movement has lacked almost totally in those constructive elements which we meet with in similar movements in other countries, such as Denmark or Ireland. Never have I seen in any Swadeshi literature the wish expressed to preserve Indian manufactures on account of their intrinsic excellence, or because the presence amongst us of these highly skilled craftsmen represented an important element in the national culture, or because these craftsmen still worked under conditions of life still infinitely superior, physically and spiritually, to those of the European factory-slaves.

Too often the leaders of our political movement have forgotten (as men forgot in the early days of the development of European industrialism) that elementary principle of statecraft, that *men are of more account than things.* They have forgotten that the goal of all material civilisation is not labour but leisure, and that industry without art only brutalises and degrades. For *things* then—things economic, political, temporary—they have been willing to undermine both our immemorial industrial culture, and to degrade the status and destroy the physique of those artisans who once served us so faithfully and who even now if we would let them would make our cities and our houses beautiful again. I know no sign more ominous for the future of the Indian civilisation, than our utter indifference to social industrial idealism, and the heartless callousness with which we have cast aside the services of those who built our homes, and clothed and wrought for us in the days before we learned to despise our own culture,—leaving them to eke out a precarious living by making petty trivialities for tourists, curio-collectors, and for Anglo-Indian bungalows, or to drift into the ranks of menial labourers or factory hands. Do you think that we can thus degrade the status of so many men without impairing the vitality of our national life and without injuring the basis of its possible prosperity?

We, who think that we are educated and progressive, we, who attend conferences and sit on legislative councils, who are rulers of states, or earn more princely incomes in courts of law, we ourselves have despised and hated everything Indian, and it is by that hatred that we have destroyed our industries and degraded the status of our artisans. And when at last our pockets were touched—then so far from realising what we had done, we set ourselves to form Swadeshi companies for making enamelled cufflinks (with pansies on them), for dyeing yarn (with German dyes), or making uncomfortable furniture (for Anglo-Indians). We never thought that the fault was in ourselves. We lived in caricatured English villas, and studied the latest fashion in collars and ties and sat on the verandahs of Collectors bungalows and strove to preserve our respectability by listening to gramophone records of the London music halls instead of living Indian singers—we learned to sit on chairs and eat with spoons and to adorn our walls with German oleographs and our floors with Brussels carpets: and then we thought to save our souls by taking shares in some Swadeshi company for making soap.

True Swadeshi is none of these things: it is a way of looking at life. It is essentially sincerity. Seek first this, learn once more the *art of living,* and you will find that our ancient civilisation, industrial no less than spiritual, will re-arise from the ashes of our vulgarity and parasitism of today.

I do not think we fully realise the depth of our present intellectual poverty. If everything produced in India during the nineteenth century were to be suddenly miraculously destroyed, the world would be very little the poorer. The creative force in us has died, because we had no faith in ourselves—we could only learn to be intellectual parasites;

to make, as has been said, of our country a mere suburb of Birmingham and Paris. It is imperative that we should recognize our real position, if we could reconstruct our national life. To this end, years of patient labour in the field of National Education is needed. So long as this education is based on the assumption that all true light and learning must come from Europe, so long will the restoration of industrial prosperity for India be impossible.

The first thing that must always strike a critical visitor examining Indian work exposed for sale in shops, or at an Industrial exhibition, is the extraordinary and consistent contrast between old and modern work. The latter almost always shows marked degeneration in respect of technique or intention or both. The place of those things which used to be common but now are rare is taken by cheap substitutes and by imitations of the imported superfluities of European over-production. The most significant phenomenon is the change of application of all the more elaborate arts, such as enamelling, wood carving, and embroidery, from the real service of the daily needs, domestic and ceremonial, of the people of the country, to the production of trinkets and curiosities for tourists and foreign markets. It is this fact which accounts for an often criticised feature in the modern work—the faulty construction or over-loading of ornaments which are so often combined with patient and devoted labour and the use of fine and traditional designs. One may instance the ill-fitting hinges of inlaid glove boxes: the elaborate carving of the tops of tables, making them useless *as tables,* exquisite embroidery for blouses applied to cheap materials which do not last, or worked in colours which do not wash. This state of affairs results from the facts that the craftsman does not use, and has little or nothing to do with persons who do use, glove-boxes, tables, and blouses, and there can be no serious change in the position of the Industrial arts of India until the present *Indian* boycott of the *Indian* craftsman is replaced by something more like that intelligent boycott of worthless importations from Europe (and their imitations made in India) which Lord Curzon so passionately advocated at Delhi.

No less than forty years ago Sir George Birdwood wrote "Indian Native Gentlemen and Ladies should make it a point of culture never to wear any clothing or ornaments but of native manufacture and strictly native design." How we should have scoffed at this idea then! Even now there are Bengali gentlemen who bring home trunks full of English dresses for their wives after completing their studies at the English bar: and it is not ten years since the students of the Calcutta School of Art went on strike, and were strongly supported in doing so by the Bengali press, because an Englishman dared to think that real Indian art instead of second rate European might be made the basis of the teaching in the school. It is true that things have changed during the last ten years, and a change once begun progresses swiftly: but the amount of change is still insignificant, and we are only to a small extent less parasitic than the last generation. It is a marvel to me how any self-respecting people can endure for a day, not the system of government,—but the system of education from which we suffer, a system which is a far deeper and more perpetual insult to our culture than any of the incidents in railway trains of which we hear so much. The Education Court at the late United Provinces Exhibition, for instance was little more than a gigantic advertisement of English schoolmasters and Messrs Macmillan. There was practically nothing Indian about it. It is not surprising that the products of such education do not care for Indian art. It would be more surprising if they did.

Let me now briefly analyse the chief causes of decline in Indian industrial art.

Every one knows that architecture is a synthesis of all the arts and that their prosperity is bound up with that of the art of building. Modern Indian architecture* however, domestic or palatial, is at the very lowest ebb. The average modern house is a cross between a suburban villa and a Government barrack. The new palaces of most of the rulers of native States are, as Sir George Birdwood has remarked, like anything in the world except a habitation fit for kings. While European architecture is nominally the model, in India, "the essence of European architecture is supposed to consist in a reckless disregard of all recognized canons of ornament and proportion".

It is very true, as Mr. Lockwood Kipling remarked in the first volume of the *Journal of Indian Art*—"It is on the architecture of today that the preservation of Indian Art semblance of healthy life now hinges." Yet so far as I am aware it has never occurred to any Swadeshist politician to demand from Government that in public buildings Indian architecture should be the rule, and Indian architects employed or that the State should again patronise and foster Indian artistic industries. These things are still done in some of the native States: but not in all of these—Baroda, for instance, affords a conspicuously objectionable example of Anglicisation and total disregard of Indian artistic tradition. Nearly everywhere in India there are still living hereditary and most capable working architects—such as no other country in the world still possesses—but like other craftsmen they are being starved by neglect and forced to adopt menial or agricultural work for a bare living.

Living in pseudo-European homes naturally and logically involves and corresponds to the using of European furniture,

* I.e., architecture as seen in the modern cities and as patronised by the 'English educated'. In many parts of India a very fine tradition of building still survives; but it is being killed by neglect.

clothes and finally, to an entire dependence on imported apparatus of material comfort and amusement—a dependence upon boxes of sardines and upon gramophones and on all that lies between them. In this process an accelerating touch is given by employing slightly educated Eurasian governesses to teach our daughters the use of knives and forks.

I should like to say in passing, that in speaking thus I do not mean in any way to disparage things European, as such. Nothing is further from my thoughts than that absurd notion which is expressed in the not uncommon saying, "that *our* ancestors were civilised when Europeans were 'dressed' in woad." As a matter of fact early Keltic and Teutonic Europe was much more civilised in some respects than we are today—at least it cared more for creative and imaginative art. What I do wish to point out is that *our imitations,* whether in Swadeshi factories or in our lives, of things European are and must always be for ourselves socially and industrially disintegrating, and for the rest of the world wholly valueless.

Nor do I mean that we should never assimilate or adopt any foreign idea or custom. On the contrary I believe that even in such things as music and the plastic arts, and still more in sociology we have some things to learn from others, as well as to recover from our own past: only we do not show our progress in these things by taking to harmoniums, by buying German oleographs, or by adopting the crudest and least considered phases of a foreign culture. But let us recognise that by doing these things we offend both against the higher and the lower ideal of Swadeshi—the higher which is in our hearts, and the lower in our pockets.

Let us now study the process of disintegration further, passing from architecture, the main setting of our lives, to all the lesser elements of our environment.

"Not in Benares only" says Sir G. Watt, "but throughout India the fine old art designs that have been attained after centuries of evolution are being abandoned and models utterly unsuited and far inferior artistically are being substituted. The writer can confidently affirm that he found in at least fifty percent of the important silversmiths shops in India, the illustrated trade catalogues of European firms and stores being employed as the pattern books upon which their silver plate was being modelled." The natural result is that when you want a Polo Trophy, you have to go to England for it—for we know that our Swadeshi imitations of European industrial art are never as good as the originals and are never likely to be. Swadeshi as we *now* understand it—i.e., erecting factories for naturalising European manufactures—is simply accepting for ourselves a permanent inferiority of environment, and irremediably lowering the standard of living amongst us.

The modern amongst us can already tolerate an environment of cheap hideousness and tawdry, expensive discomfort, which would have disgusted the poorest in the days of Hindu or Mughal civilisation.

Take Benares brass: at Delhi "all but one or two pieces were bad in design and worse in execution."

Take enamelling: "Formerly every attention was given to effect, and a background or field colour was regularly employed, most frequently a rich creamy white. Within the past few decades this has been discontinued, and complex and intricate designs substituted in which it can hardly be said there is a field colour at all. The result is distinctly inferior and may be described as garish rather than artistic."

A Benares Kinkhab manufacturer, asked to show a treasured pattern book, produced a sample book of English wall papers—"This at once explained the monstrous degeneration perceived in the Benares Kinkhabs."

The value of gold thread imported into India is now 44 lacs. It is much inferior to India handmade gold thread, now going out of use. The author of a monograph on Indian Gold lace remarks: "In such seemingly minor and unimportant details the true cause of the artistic degeneracy of Indian weaving is to be found."

Exactly the same conclusion may be drawn from the imports of aniline dyes. In such cases we actually pay money out of pocket, to ruin our own industrial arts.

It would be useless to multiply examples here: those who wish may find them in the pages of all, Indian or English, who have written upon the industrial arts of India. I think no one will deny that these Industrial arts are in a nearly hopeless state. No one can ultimately deny that the main cause of this is our own deficient artistic understanding. It is, I repeat, far more necessary to cease our own boycott of the Indian craftsman, than for us to carry on a boycott of foreign imports.

In attempting to establish factories for the imitation of European imported goods we overlook one thing—the relative value of men and things. True Swadeshi would have attempted to preserve the status of our skilled artisans and village craftsmen, for the sake of the value to our country of men *as men.* Already it is being recognized in Europe that the general substitution of machines for men must invariably lower the whole intellectual and moral status of the working population: and we need not hope to avoid this result by tinkering at compulsory education. A False Swadeshi does not object to crowding the craftsmen into factories, where drunkenness, physical degeneration and all other natural results of the factory system follow. One has but to read the reports of factory inspectors to understand—"The legal hours of rest for women are constantly exceeded:" "sanitary arrangements are horrible:" "children are often puny, probably owing to overwork." "Nearly every factory is a constant offender." Such are the facts recorded in the last report of the Director of Industries in the Punjab. The moral should be clear. Yet we find the members of the late

Factory Commission lamenting the absence of a pure factory class, totally severed from village life, in Western India. The whole endeavour of a True Swadeshi should be to restore, not to destroy, the organic life of the village communities. It is not that we learn too much from foreign countries. We learn too little. If we learnt more, we should not want to repeat the experiments in *Laissez faire* of early Victorian England.

To sum up our conclusions—

Who are the natural patrons of our Industrial Arts? Not tourists, I think you will agree. The sumptuary arts of India, the decline of which we are discussing, are those which naturally most depend, like architecture itself, on the tastes and patronage of the educated, aristocratic and wealthy classes amongst us and of the courts and have always so depended: and unless we can restore the fine aesthetic culture which these classes in India once possessed, we cannot hope that our Industrial Arts will flourish. Mr. Burns the other day remarked that out of two hundred wedding presents which he had the opportunity of seeing at an Indian wedding, only some sixteen were Indian in point of character and origin: and the same state of affairs may be observed in the houses of almost all our prosperous lawyers and Deputy Collectors. Now the situation is this—that a mere desire to save money for our country will never remedy this state of affairs, neither will a wish to achieve political revenge. But artistic education, the setting of men before things in our own estimation, and the ideal of nationality as service may achieve, what lesser motives cannot. What is necessary is that we should let the real love of our country allow us to realize that Her gifts are (with the rarest exceptions) really and intrinsically better than those which we can import—that our dyes, our handmade gold thread, our designs, our ways of dressing and building, our jewellery, our carpets and all that goes to make the daily environment of our lives are better than the things we import from Europe—more beautiful, more enduring, more vital in response and more a part of our real life. Then it will not be so difficult perhaps to spend a little more in the first instance on such things. But all this is not a matter of political platforms, it is simply and solely a matter of National Education, the sort of education that will help us some day to prefer a living singer to what an Indian friend of mine has very aptly called 'the voice of the living dead'. Then we shall be saved not only the expense of importing gramophones, but all the bother of trying to make them in local factories, with indifferent success. This is a parable of all the other Industrial Arts.

Secondly, the great manufacturers can take care of themselves. Business men will not fail to discover where money can be made. It is hardly necessary for us to assist them in becoming millionaires by bringing to their aid the whole weight of Swadeshi sentimentality. We have only to see that they injure as little as possible the physique and morale of the workers. Temporary cheapness is no guarantee of ultimate value from the standpoint of national evolution or even of private advantage on the part of the individual purchaser. Swadeshi does not consist in imitating new productions recently imported,—this may be left to the speculative businessman, who has his due place—but in restoring the status and the prosperity of the skilled artisan and the village craftsman. It is these artisans who most need the help of our national idealism. It is these skilled craftsmen also whom we as a nation most need as members of our body politic. We have enough of agricultural labourers and are like to have too many factory hands, and perhaps too many lawyers and clerks. To assist the skilled artisan and the village craftsman may seem too simple, too unromantic a thing for nationalists to undertake. Even national education requires half a century to bear its fruits. Yet it is assuredly only by such personal activity and gradual recovery of social co-operation that an end so great as the restoration of our status amongst the nations of the world can be achieved. And it is almost waste of time to work for ends that may or may not be achieved in ten or fifteen years: the greatest work is done by those who scarcely look to see its fruits within their own lifetime.

# 3

## Domestic Handicraft and Culture*

Let me begin with definitions. Once upon a time all handicrafts were domestic. It would not be far wrong to say that none now are so. But for the purpose of these notes I shall consider as domestic handicrafts those which have been, historically speaking, most generally practised in the home: it will be convenient to take spinning and weaving as the typical case, to stand for all the home industries which have been swept away by modern industrialism. I shall expressly exclude from consideration any mere accomplishments such as modern education commonly substitutes, especially in the case of women, for real and practical knowledge. The dabbler in fretwork, enamelling, or book-binding, who merely earns pin-money and undersells the trade, I shall also ignore. But the serious practice of a craft such as jewellery or book-binding under small workshop conditions stand nearly in the same relation to culture as the practice of an actually domestic craft, and should be considered, especially when the small workshop is in or near the home, so that the work going on becomes part of the everyday experience of the family.

To define culture is perhaps a harder thing. Plato identified it with the capacity for immediate and instinctive discrimination between good and bad workmanship, of whatever sort; it is perhaps in this respect that the present age is least of all cultivated. We may expand this definition by including a certain quality of recollectedness or detachment, a capacity for

*Lecture read before the Association of Teachers of Domestic Science, London, May 1910.

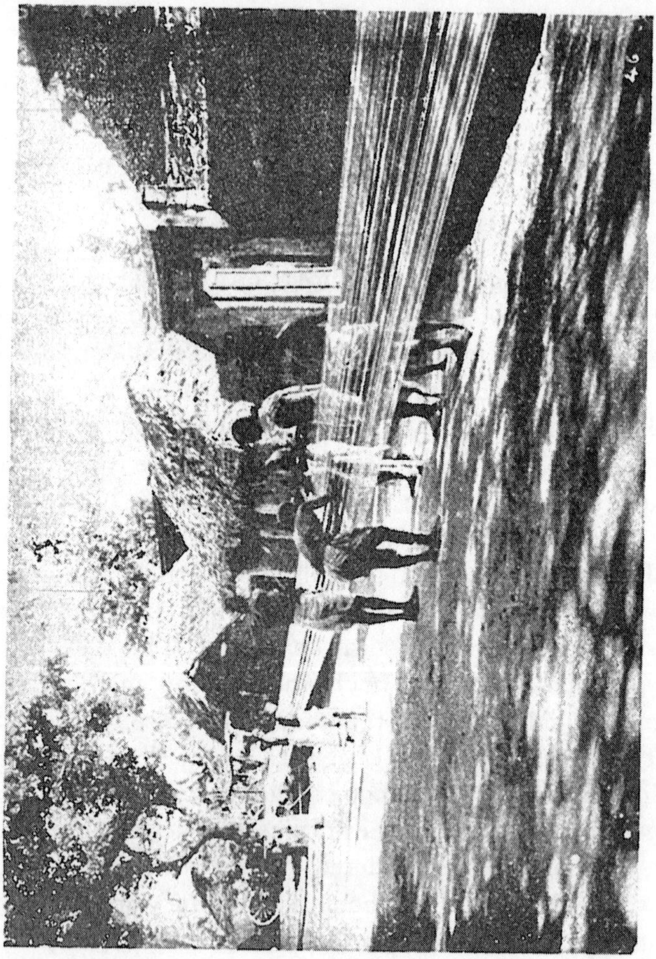

Pl. I. Weavers in the Streets, Tanjore

stillness of mind and body (restlessness is essentially uncultured), and the power of penetrating mere externals in individual men or various races. Culture includes a view of life essentially balanced, where real and false values are not confused; also, I think, a certain knowledge of, or interest in, things which are not directly utilitarian, that is to say, which do not merely give pleasure to the senses or confirm a prejudice. If these things, or some of them, be culture, how does the practice of a domestic craft such as weaving (which we have chosen as the type) stand in relation to them?

If you could walk through the streets of an Eastern town, or through the streets of London as they must have been a few centuries ago, you would find life and handicraft very much more intimately associated than is now the case. You would see weaving, shoemaking, metal-work, carpentry and many other crafts all going forward as part of the common life. And when such conditions as these obtained, every body possessed a more general knowledge of the ways in which things were done, and they actually did very much more for themselves. Together with this, went a more real knowledge of the qualities of materials, and the instinctive demand that they should be useful as well as attractive superficially. Under such conditions it was not as easy as it now is to pass off inferior wool, bad jam, and flimsy furniture upon the thrifty housewife, for she knew how to spin the wool, to make the jam, and her brother or a neighbour was the carpenter. Whatever may or may not have been gained by transferring the centre of production from the home to the factory, it is very clear that certain things have been lost. It is perhaps mainly a result of this non-acquaintance with the conditions of production that is accountable for the small respect in which workmanship is now held, and above all for the persistent demand for cheap pretentious goods on the part of those who formerly possessed solid and durable things.

Under domestic conditions, whatever is made is made to fulfil its purposes. Under industrial conditions, nearly everything that is made is made primarily for sale at a profit, and it is almost a matter of indifference if the ostensible purpose of the goods be effectively attained.

There are scarcely any objects associated with our daily home life, which are not better made, in respect of quality, by hand than by machine. As I look around my study, I see nothing for which I have to thank mechanical production under factory conditions. I know well that no machine, not one of a thousand factories, can make for me a rug as fine as the unlettered wandering tribes of Central Asia can still weave in their own tents. No steam saw or mechanism for machine carving can design my settee, or make my chair or table as I would have it. No photographs of the works of the great masters compensate me for the absence of a living art that could have built a modern house as beautiful in mass and detail as is the old one I am fortunate enough to live in. And of books, the best are centuries old, or are the product of modern hand-presses under small workshop conditions. Machinery, in fact, has not enriched our home life. Even if it has brought to us the treasures of the ends of the earth, we have a heavy price to pay for these, nothing less than the destruction of such art at its very sources. The effect of substituting mechanical for domestic and small workshop production has really been this, that certain fine things which used to be obtainable in every market-place in the world are now only to be seen in museum. Because they are to be seen in museums, we imagine that we are cultured. But by their fruits we shall know them. We know by their work that men of old were cultivated. What will future generations, judging by our works, think of us? For, as Watts once said, "scarcely a single object amongst those that surround us, has any pretension to real beauty, or could be put simply into a picture with noble effect." How does this affect our culture? Let us return to Plato. There is in all these things, such as weaving, he says, propriety and impropriety; and we must restrain the "ill, undisciplined, illiberal, indecent" manner, "lest our guardians, being educated in the midst of ill-representations, as in an ill pasture, whereby everyday plucking and eating a deal of different things, by little and little they contract imperceptibly some mighty evil in their souls."

When we consider the restlessness which characterises modern life, we need go no further to enquire what that evil may be. To be satisfied with imitations—to be able to endure a gramophone after once hearing a living singer—to walk upon a carpet covered with bunches of roses tied in ribbons—to call "art paper" a paste of China clay used for reproducing photographic illustrations in cheap books—for women in their dress to deform their internal organs and their feet—for men to use by preference dingy tubular garments best adapted not to show the dirt of the atmosphere they are content to breathe—to place imitative dexterity in art above the power of great invention or nobility of motif—to assume superiority of soul on the mere ground of increased empirical knowledge—to accept always the report of the senses against the report of intuition—to seek always for novelty—these things are the opposite of culture, and some of them are caused by, or made possible by the destruction of the domestic crafts. Perhaps it would be truer to say that both things, our loss of culture and the destruction of handicraft, result from some inner malady which we do not comprehend; but even if this be so, we cannot fail to recognise the close connection between the actual phenomena. Restlessness is born of idleness. Thought is stimulated by rhythmic (but not unintelligent) labour. When the senses are, as it were, told off to carry on their own work, then the mind awakens to ideas. I do not think that women are wiser because they have abandoned the spinning wheel and the loom for the office and the factory. I think they have lost reflectiveness. One does not forget that the childhood of Christ was spent in a carpenter's shop, nor that two at least of India's greatest poets and religious teachers—Kabir and Tiruvalluvar—were weavers. I cannot think of any instance where the destruction of a handicraft has promoted culture. We should consider whether men or things are the greatest possession of a nation.

The subject of this address is Handicraft and Culture with special reference to the home. The home we may take in its broadest sense to mean all that part of our environment which is personal and intimate, as distinguished from that which is merely temporary and utilitarian. In these personal things mechanism overreaches itself. It attains too great an uniformity in methods and materials. Dyes, stained glass, enamels, all these become too uniform. Machine planed wood, a steam-impressed book-binding have no vitality of surface. No one can make a violin as well as they were made two centuries ago in little workshops. From the standpoint of culture, is there any compensation for this to be found in our increased material comfort, or in mere variety and novelty?

The actual making of machinery itself is almost the only living craft—where excellence in the craft itself is a first consideration. It is not machinery that we need to abandon in our search for culture. We could ill spare the culture of the electrician, the engineer and the builder of bridges. All that we need is to use, not to misuse the power these men can give us. Let me illustrate by an example the relation of machinery to handicraft and culture. Take such a trade as carpet-making under modern conditions, by powerlooms. The operator has no longer to design, or to weave in and out the threads with his own fingers. He is employed in reality, not as a carpet weaver—such men no longer exist—but as the tender of a machine. He may, it is true, rise to a higher place, but it is only the place of a man responsible for the successful running of many machines by many men. He can never rise by virtue of his knowledge or experience in the craft itself, because, as I have said, the craft no longer exists. The craftsman himself can always, if allowed to, draw the delicate distinction between the machine and the tool. The carpet loom is a tool, a contrivance for holding warp threads at a stretch, for the pile to be woven round them by the craftsmen's fingers; but the powerloom is a machine, and its significance as a destroyer of culture lies in the fact that it does the essentially human part of the work and imposes limitations on the spontaneity and freedom of the design and the imagination of the worker. These limitations react upon the user in the form of lifelessness, lack of temperament or response, in his daily environment.

I should like you to consider carefully the effect upon us of the nature of our daily environment. We all of us believe more or less in what we call association, we are sensitive to the personal impress surviving in the relics of great men, the books they possessed or the letters they wrote; and we should agree that no reproduction, however theoretically perfect, could ever have a value equal to that of the authentic work of a master's own hand. A beautiful description of an Indian lute, in the *Arabian Nights,* tells us that when its strings were touched, it sang of the waters that gave it drink, and the earth whence it sprang, of the carpenters who cut it and the polishers who polished it and the merchants who made it their merchandise, and the ships that shipped it. And which of us, who seek to surround ourselves with the work of human hands and hearts, is deaf to what the nomad carpet tells us of life in Central Asian tents, to what the moulded stone and adze-cut beam inform us the mediaeval builder, or the Saxon jewel of its wearer? Are we not also sensitive to the inventive force and loving care expressed in the work of modern craftsmen, in a volume from the Kelmscott Press or a painted chest from Daneway House? And if we lacked this sensitiveness, should we not lack just so much culture? But you cannot eat your cake and have it. Everything was once made in that personal individual way. We cannot keep that sensitiveness in a purely mechanical environment.

One of those men who are best described as born travellers, lately remarked that the Burman "if asked to give his candid opinion after a year's experience of English life, would probably say that the position of the vast majority of Englishmen was not much better than that of chained slaves." And would the Burman be far wrong? I think not. For if it were a legal punishment for serious crime that a man should spend ten hours out of every twenty-four in a hole in the ground clipping tiny pieces out of small cards, or that a man should spend his days adding figures at a desk, I am sure that some of us of the Humanitarian League would have much to say of the barbaric cruelty of our prison system. It is only, I think, because men are now so accustomed to the idea of doing unintelligent work, that they can be got to perform such tasks as these.

There has lately been a great revival of appreciation of folk-music. How much of this music do you think is the product of factory conditions, and how much belongs to hand work and to the open air? What is the use of patronising an art like this, if the very structure of our society is for ever destroying the possibility of its continued growth?

The forces destroying culture move in a vicious circle. No individual ever made a gramophone because he loved music; but the gramophones made in factories are daily destroying the capacity for appreciating real music in the villages. I know of one Cotswold village where the local shopkeeper has no less than twenty gramophones hired out in the local public houses, where men used once to sing themselves.

I have already alluded to one other phase of the relation between industrialism and culture. I mean the destruction of culture in other, particularly Asiatic countries, as the result of mechanical over-production in Europe. As William Morris wrote: "the Indian or Javanese craftsman may no longer ply his craft leisurely, working a few hours a day, in producing a maze of strange beauty on a piece of cloth; a steam engine is set a-going at Manchester, and that victory over Nature and a thousand stubborn difficulties is used for the base work of producing a sort of plaster of China clay and shoddy, and the Asiatic worker, if he is not starved to death outright, as plentifully happens, is driven himself into a factory to lower the wages of his Manchester brother, and nothing of character is left him except, most like, an accumulation of fear and hatred of that to him unaccountable evil, his English master." Perhaps the extraordinary meanness of the English or Dutch manufacturer who sponges on Indian or Javanese design, and reproduces mechanical and very inferior imitations of it very cheaply for the European or for the local Asiatic market has not struck you! The process is often described as "successfully contesting the village weaver's market." I shall not be so foolish as to suggest the governing of European manufacture by ethical considerations, for there is better work to do at present than such a ploughing of the sand. I do, however, wish to point out that the solidarity of humanity, especially under modern conditions of easy transport, is too real to permit of such causes failing to react for the worse upon European culture.

In conclusion, therefore, I suggest to you that the substitution of mechanical production under factory conditions, for hand production under domestic or small workshop conditions, of such things as form the daily environment of our ordinary lives, is directly destructive of culture. For such things (mark the words such things—I do not mean everything) are better made under these conditions: their making is in itself educational—kindergartens are only necessary because these crafts have been subtracted from life; they make for rhythm and stability in our environment. Their preservation or restoration is theoretically justifiable, because under such conditions the necessity for earning a livelihood and the force of the creative instinct are the dominating factors, whereas, under wholesale industrial conditions, every other consideration is sacrificed to profit-making. Particularly I suggest that everywhere and always the competition between a man and a machine is destructive of culture. A civilisation which cannot effect between them a reasonable division of labour, does not deserve the name. The place of machinery in a true civilisation should be that of a servant, and not a master. It should carry out the simplest and most mechanical processes of manufacture, it should save the craftsman from the heaviest and least interesting part of his work; but it should not rob him of that part of his labour which is his very craft. For if it does so rob him, not only is his own intelligence correspondingly destroyed, but the community has to accept an environment aesthetically and spiritually inferior, an environment that certainly does not express or produce what we understand by culture.

The problem is not how to abolish machinery, but how so to regulate it that it shall serve without enslaving man; how to stop competition between machine and hand work by defining and delimiting intelligently the proper sphere of each. The community cannot afford to dispense with the intellectual and imaginative forces, the educational and ethical factors in life which go with the existence of skilled craftsmen and small workshops. These must therefore—if we value culture—be protected in their proper sphere. The means to this end are the endowment of craftsmanship, and the transference of the control of production from the hands of those who exploit, again into the hands of those who themselves create. Without this we must, as a race, be condemned to "polish brass and iron hour after hour, laborious work, kept ignorant of their use:" to "spend the days of wisdom in sorrowful drudgery to obtain a scanty pittance of bread, in ignorance to view a small portion and think that All, and call it demonstration blind to the simple rules of life."

# 4

# The International Congress of Applied Chemistry 1901: and Aniline Dyes

In a recent article with the above title, Prof. P.C. Ray contrasts the Indian with the German attitude to science, and taking the case of the discovery of alizarin dyes, explains what arduous labour is needed to prepare the way for such developments of new industries. "Germany" he says "is today reaping a rich harvest, it is because of the unselfish, devoted and whole-hearted labours of generations of chemists for nearly a century." The result of these labours has "revolutionised one of our leading industries, and completely destroyed a stable trade of France, Holland, Italy and Turkey" (and the East). "The cultivation of the various species of the Rubiaceae for the purpose of the dyer, which has continued for thousands of years down to our own times is now practically at an end." No question is raised as to the desirability, or otherwise, of this revolution in the dyer's methods and resources.

Let us look beneath the surface. We shall find a useful probe in one of the Platonic dialogues. In Plato's *Phaedus,* a self-confident inventor (of the art of writing) appears before the King of Egypt, but the inventor is not received with open arms. The King replies, in fact: "O most ingenious Theuth, one person is able to give birth to art, another to judge of what amount of detriment or advantage it will be to those who use it." Will it be amiss if we should enquire of the "most ingenious" scientist what amount of detriment or advantage there may be in the invention of these chemical dyes?

We may draw up a balance sheet. On the debit side we should have to set the dislocation of dying industries all over the world, and their replacement by factory work. The general effect of this process, in the aggregate, upon the physique and character of many millions of human beings has, like all changes, whether necessary or not, been enormous. Such changes and such results may sometimes be a necessary part of a progress towards a more secure, because more conscious civilisation. But they are not always so, and if the "ingenious men's" inventions are always accepted at their own valuation, are not likely to be always so. Consider the result in this case. Admittedly the object of dyeing goods is to make them beautiful; for many thousand years men have sought and won from nature the secret of her beautiful dyes, madder indigo and the rest. Now all these "natural" dyes are being superseded by the manufactured ones. Are the latter then more beautiful? Not at all. All artists, that is all that part of humanity whose sense of colour is most perfect, are agreed that the aniline dyes are almost always coarse and gaudy compared with the dyes they have replaced; it is also well-known that they are less permanent, and also that when they fade, the faded colour is particularly ugly, whereas the old dyes may be said to grow mellow, than to fade with age. A ghastly uniformity of colour is also established all over the world—a few cheap greens and reds imported in large quantities from Germany have destroyed innumerable shades and varieties of colour belonging to each district and even to each family of dyers. On the other hand, the immense resources of the chemist—more than half a thousand different synthetic dyes are already available—have enabled manufacturers to flood the market with such infinite varieties of shades of dyed silks and other raw materials as to make reasonable selection impossible.

To quote the authoritative words of a great European dye-master:

"Of these (aniline) dyes, it must be enough to say that their discovery, while conferring the greatest honour on the abstract science of chemistry, and while doing great service to capitalists in their hunt after profits, has terribly injured the art of dyeing, and for the general public has nearly destroyed it as an art."

What a grand achievement for science, what a mark of high civilisation is this!

It is not to the point to suggest (even if true) that beautiful colour *can* be produced by the use of aniline dyes, and *can* be made permanent. It is not the object of manufacturers to achieve their ends: they are incompatible with moneymaking on a large scale.

The introduction of refined and exact chemical methods has had the same disastrous effect on other arts, such as enamelling, stained glass, and indirectly of course on all the textile arts such as weaving, carpet making, and cotton printing. In all these arts, the exploitation of chemical discoveries has rendered the true practice of art increasingly difficult, and has enormously reduced the sum total of beauty available in daily life. It is a melancholy reflection, that such should be, in so many directions, the reward of modern science.

The significance of all this was foreshadowed in the story of the fall of man. Years ago, in mediaeval Europe, in India, and throughout the world under pre-Industrial conditions, the public had perforce to accept good art, good design, good colouring, (as Adam had to accept the garden of Eden) because nothing worse was available. Art was in the hands of hereditary specialists, whose simple methods produced the results which cannot be rivalled at the present day. Now Industrialism has placed an ignorant public at the mercy of exploiting manufacturers, who care nothing for art, but everything for dividends.

This process was probably necessary for progress. The choice of good and evil had to be presented in order that good might in the end be consciously chosen. The recognition of this fact should lead us to choose this good as soon and as consciously as possible. But we have not yet progressed very far.

What after all is the aim of civilisation? Do we wish to heighten or degrade our finer sensibilities? Should we wish in the end to raise all men to that capacity of understanding colour which now belongs to the few, or should we wish to degrade to the common level of indifference, these few artists that remain like prophets in spite of us? Are we to place the possibility of material wealth for some—with its loss by others—above the true ideal of civilisation, the making possible of civilised life? I think rather, that as Mrs. J.C. Bose has put it in speaking of the education of Indian women, "In making our demand for greater and deeper education and material well-being, then, may we never forget to say, But will this wealth bring me Realisation?"

If this fundamental ideal of Indian culture be applied to the problem before us, the issues clearly resolve themselves. We see that in such ways as this of increasing reliance on artificial dyes we are spending money for that which is not bread. Any true artist would far rather forego the use of dyes altogether, than continually injure his finer sensibilities by living amongst ugly and glaring colours, or amongst unhealthy and morbid imitations of faded natural dyes. It is only lack of education and lack of culture that make it possible.

Meanwhile, with the progress of scientific discovery, with the accumulation of resources which we seem able only to misuse, an enormous mass of true knowledge of rational, useful science is being daily lost.

"The art of dyeing is still in a rude state in India as far as the methods adopted are concerned, yet in looking at the results which are attained they cannot be despised even by the scientific dyeing of the West. But in the management of colours, the skill with which a number are employed, and the taste with which they are harmonised, whether in their cottons their carpets, their silks or their shawls, Europe has nothing to teach but a great deal to learn." (H.H. Cole).

"Uneducated natives may be found in almost every Indian bazar who can make alloys, colour glass, and work enamels by methods which are unknown in Europe." (Dr. Royle).

It is significant that at the Chemical Congress referred to in Prof. Ray's paper an important address dealt with this very point. Prof. Witt of Berlin, in an address to the Combined Sections of the Congress, pleaded eloquently for a study of the old empirical methods before these were lost entirely to humanity. "We have," he said "living empiricism at our door, which we allow to die and to sink into oblivion, without attempting to study it and to learn the lesson it has to teach—a treasure of information of incalculable magnitude hoarded up in the course of centuries by the skill and patience of countless millions of men who were, and are, as keen in the study of nature as they are reluctant to draw general conclusions from their observations.

"This great treasure is the industrial experience of the Eastern nations. It is an undoubted fact, and if it were not, a single visit to the South Kensington Museum would prove it, that the people of Persia, India, China, Japan, the inhabitants of Burma, Siam, Cambodia, and the innumerable islands of the Pacific, are possessed of methods for the treatment and utilisation of the products of nature which are in many cases equal, if not superior, to our own. These methods must be to a large extent based upon chemical principles. Is it not strange that we know so little about them, and that little generally only indirectly through the accounts of travellers who were not chemists? If all these peculiar methods were fully known and described by persons who have seen them applied and watched their application with the eyes of a chemist, it would certainly be not only of interest, but also of the greatest utility to our own industry; for it is the elucidation of empirical methods which, in the new light that science sheds upon them, leads to new departures and to progress."

In this direction Prof. Ray himself has done invaluable service in the two admirable volumes on the history of Hindu chemistry which we owe to him. But there is room for much more to be done; and those who would truly serve their country and serve humanity, will devote themselves rather to the preservation of old arts and industries, than to the exploitation of new methods without regard to their true human and ultimate value. We need science, and above all concrete efficiency; but it is not *any* science or *any* efficiency that will help us, only a rational and humane science, and efficiency directed to high ends.

The discovery of aniline dyes may be due to the unselfish devoted labours of generations of chemists but even so, it does not follow that there is anything "unselfish," though there may be "whole-hearted devotion" (to money), in the capitalist's exploitation of the scientific *kalpa-druma*. Science will be able to produce for us as many modern miracles as we desire. So long as we regard these as the end and justification of science, we remain but an evil generation, demanding signs, and bent on mere material well-being. But this will not be progress, nor civilisation. Do not then let us hold up to Young India an ideal of industrial science of an indiscriminating character. Let us learn rather to live than accumulate the means of living. Let us rather learn to refine our wants, to increase sensitiveness, than to multiply our wants and blunt our finer instincts.

# 5

## The Function of Schools of Art in India: A Reply to Mr. Cecil Burns

In the *Journal of the Society of Arts* for June, 1909, there is printed a lecture delivered before the society in London on May, 27th, by Mr. Cecil Burns, Principal of the Sir Jamsetjee Jeejeebhoy School of Art in Bombay.

The whole matter is of great importance in relation to the economic future of India, and the moral and intellectual significance and value of Indian Nationalism, for India and for the world.

I know nothing whatever directly of Mr. Burns himself. It seems to me that he speaks as one who is sincere enthusiastic, and well-intentioned; but I think that he, and his pupils, are equally victims of a system and a point of view which are likely to continue in the future as in the past, to destroy the possibility of sincerity, imagination and individuality in art, whether in Europe or in India.

I have twice visited the Bombay Schools of Art, and on each occasion was impressed with the entire lack of inspiration, the dreary futility of nearly all that was going on. The whole *regime,* from ideals to methods, like the education provided in Missionary schools and contemplated in official universities, was so entirely un-Indian as to explain at once the dullness of the results. It is the irony of fate that the one School of Art built and endowed by an Indian, should be the least Indian in aims and methods.

Mr. Burns' own acquaintance with Indian art seems to be entirely academic. I do not remember that there was a single good Indian painting on the walls of the school. However, I may illustrate the point by a reference to jewellery. No one possessing any serious knowledge of Indian jewellery could speak "of the massive proportions and primitive character of Indian jewellery." Mr. Burns is probably acquainted only with such jewellery as he has seen in museums, where anthropologists collect together whatever is primitive and barbarous, to the exclusion of what is refined and delicate. It is nonsense to talk of the "lighter and more delicate styles of workmanship of Europe." There are still hundreds of goldsmiths in India who can execute fine work in gold, such as few, perhaps no European craftsman could imitate. Sir George Birdwood, indeed, long ago contrasted the delicate workmanship of Indian jewellery, where the cost of workmanship is in very high proportion to that of the value of the materials, with the much heavier and clumsier English jewellery, valued mainly for its intrinsic worth. Amongst the Indian peoples, there are races in many different stages of culture, and it is observable that Anglo-Indians usually study and generalise from those of the lower types. Mr. Burns appears to have gathered his ideas of Indian jewellery from the hill tribes. The goldsmith of Southern India, or the enameller of Jaipur has much more to teach than to learn in a School of Art—and I have heard art teachers in England express their desire to get such teachers if they could.

Mr. Burns, again, complains of the mixture of baser metals with Indian silver, and contrasts this state of affairs with the 'hallmarking' at Goldsmith's Hall in London, which guarantees the quality of English plate. Now, although Mr. Burns admits that "the European visitor has been the means of encouraging the faults most noticeable in the Indian silversmiths," he does not quite realise the significance of the degradation of standard he refers to. Perhaps the following story will explain that significance better—"Formerly," says Sir George Birdwood, "a great industry in gold-embroidered shoes flourished at Lucknow. They were in demand all over India, for the native Kings of Oudh would not allow the shoemakers to use any but pure gold wire on them. But when we annexed the kingdom, *all such restrictions were removed*, and the bazaars of Oudh were at once flooded with the pinchbeck embroidered shoes of Delhi, and the Lucknow shoemakers were swept away for ever by the besom of free trade." Again Sir W. Lawrence writes of Srinagar trades: "The state exercised a vigorous supervision over the quality of the raw materials and the manufactured article. In the good days of the shawl trade no spurious wool was brought in from Amritsar to be mixed with the real shawl-wool of Central Asia, and, woe betide the weaver who did bad work or the silversmith who was too liberal with his alloy. *There is no such supervision nowadays.*" Again, it is only in the *Native* State of Kashmir at the present day that the importation of aniline dyes is prohibited; everywhere else they have been allowed to do their destructive work unchecked.

Now what is this 'hallmarking' of which Mr. Burns speaks? It is nothing more than the last forlorn relic of the once universally exercised power of the English guilds to protect the standard of production; and this relic is upheld by law. There is no reason why the present rulers of India should not have continued to the trade guilds the support which they received under Indian kings; there is no reason why some guarantee of standard should not, through the still existing guilds, be enforced for Indian silverwork. There is a reason perhaps—that Englishmen do not so deeply care for the future of Indian art and industry, as to think much about the matter, but it is cruel at the same time to taunt the Indian craftsman with the degradation of his standard, as if that degradation had been of his deliberate choosing. No other causes than the withdrawal of State protection and the change in educated Indian taste (which does deserve contempt) are at the root of the evil in this case.

This change of taste is essentially snobbishness—for Indians are not content to be politically and economically dependent, but must fawn upon their rulers to the extent of Anglicising their homes and their lives. It appears to be the ambition of some to be English in all but colour. I am not surprised at Mr. Burns' statement, that out of over two hundred presents at a fashionable Indian wedding, only sixteen were of Indian origin. I should say that this eight per cent, fairly represents the 'Indianness' in the mind of a thoroughly Anglicised and 'educated' Indian of today. One other instance of Mr. Burns' apparent ignorance of Indian art. He says that in India "painting and sculpture had never been considerated except as parts of the decorative scheme of a building or some other composite work." It would take too long to show here, that this statement, which would be equally true of mediaeval Europe, is merely another way of saying that all the arts were harmonised in one great unity, based, as all art must be, on architecture. The modern method of painting pictures and sticking them indiscriminately on nails about the walls of houses comes as near perhaps to the absolute divorce of art from architecture as is possible; but it is not a sign of taste on which to congratulate the moderns. The old Indians knew better, that walls were to be painted on, and that the heart and centre of the temple was its image; and neither painting nor image were executed apart from any consideration of the place they were to occupy. But I have spoken of Mr. Burns' apparent ignorance, and in so doing I referred to the fact that he here ignores the portfolio pictures of the Mughal period in Northern India; and as he has placed none of these exquisite things on the wall of his School of Art, I am forced to suppose that he is not aware of their existence. The old

Mughal nobles had the good taste, not to dot the wall of their houses with miscellaneous pictures hanging at all angles (as they may be seen in the homes of 'educated' Indians today), but to employ the most skilled miniature painters, to paint for them pictures of the subjects traditional in North Indian culture, the portraits of kings and saints, the love of Laili and Majnuni, pictures of the chase or of war: and there are not wanting also Hindu subjects, Uma serving Mahadeva, and many a picture of the Lord of the Eternal Snows Himself. All these things, which more sympathetic and more understanding men like Mr. Havell and Mr. Percy Brown have collected in the Schools of Calcutta and Lahore and made the basis of their teaching, Mr. Burns ignores. It is only such portfolio pictures, which like a book, form in themselves a unity, that are rightly to be considered apart from architecture: but Mr. Burns informs us that painting in India was never so considered.

Two causes of the decline of Indian crafts, Mr. Burns has omitted to mention: one is the passing away of many Native Courts, as in Tanjore, where the Court was the great patron of the sumptuary arts; the other the fact that India is not a sovereign State, with Ambassadors and Consuls scattered through the world to send Home information of the true requirements of those countries with which India might still conduct, as once she did, an export trade in the products of sumptuary art.

Mr. Burns is probably right in thinking that Indian students must for a time be brought back into closer touch with nature. But are Englishmen the right men for this work? And must it not rather be by harmonising life with nature, than by merely imitating nature in a School of Art? That Indian must see with his own eyes. Two things are needful, one that he should be saturated with the traditional art of his race in order that he may know *how to see*, the other that he be saturated with the traditional culture of the East, that he may know *what to see*—for it would be meaningless to base the decorative art of a people upon rare plant forms (however beautiful) which have not appealed already to the race imagination and have no part in the race life or in their literature. All this merely goes to show that the work of truly restoring the arts and crafts of India can only be done by Indians. Englishmen can at best but help, as some have done: but some have hindered too.

Mr. Burns is afraid that Government, 'as is usual in India,' will have to show the way. Why not? As Mr Burns points out, there are thirty Schools of Art in an area of about 100 sq. miles in London, having some 400 professors and instructors. The schools are supported by public grants. I do not know why it should be otherwise in India. I only wonder whether Englishmen as a whole, really wish to revive the arts and industries of India in such an effective manner as shall enable them to compete successfully with those of England.

The ancient craft work of India is no "as dead as the art of the Greeks or of the Renaissance in Europe." Only one whose experience was confined to an Anglicised commercial, and unromantic town like Bombay, could think that. The crafts of India are, indeed, in a bad way: but they could be saved by a true national impulse, by a true Swadeshi spirit. But a Swadeshi that seeks only to boycott or imitate European manufactures, for a temporary political end will not save them : not will four Schools of Art in India, administered by men who are prepared to acquiesce without remonstrance in the official decision to adopt European styles (i.e., second-hand Gothic or third-hand Classic) in Government and other public buildings, save them any the more. Is it not, by the way, perhaps an omen, that the Victoria Memorial building in Calcutta, designed after much controversy, in the European manner, is slowly sinking in the Ganges mud?

Mr. Burns has a contempt for the way in which modern craftsmen "are content, to let their ancestors do their thinking for them." This is *one* way of looking at tradition; and perhaps there is some wisdom in giving a due place to the demand for a 'return to nature.' But the more I see of Indian Art, the more I doubt whether it ever has been so 'divorced from nature' as to make it possible to speak of a 'return.' Only the modern imitations of European wares are really divorced from nature, inasmuch as they express nothing. But while it is true that art never stands still, and it is not sufficient to teach and to copy old designs, nevertheless India is not yet, and surely never will be so changed, that the whole spirit of her decorative art must be changed too. It is much more the case that a return to nature, must be a return to sincerity and a return to nature in life itself. The arts of India must retain their Indian spirit, or become altogether worthless. The springs of art are in life itself, and when the life of the people is revitalised and reinspired, this new life will be reflected in Indian decorative art. The applied arts cannot be isolated and located as a thing apart from the national life, and the future of Indian art depends on the future of nationalism amongst us. You cannot gather grapes of thorns: and a denationalised people, an India subdued by Europe, not merely outwardly, but in her inmost self, will not produce a national art. That India is not really so subdued, that the national movement that has stirred her deepest life has a deeper significance than one that is merely political and economic, has already been proved by the development of the National School of Painting in Bengal.

But if Abanindra Nath Tagore and his followers stand in this art revival of ours, to a certain extent in the place occupied by the pre-Raphallities in the history of English art, where is our William Morris? Probably the time for his coming is not ripe. When he comes, he will do more for Indian applied art than all the schools together; but it is the function of the schools to make his path no harder than it need be.

The real difficulty at the root of all questions of Indian education is this, that modern education in India, the education which Englishmen are proud of having 'given' to India is really based on the general assumption (quite universal in England) that India is a *savage* country, which it is England's divine mission to *civilise*. This is the more or less unconscious underlying principle throughout. The facts were more truly realised by Sir Thomas Munro, when he wrote that "if civilisation were to be made an article of commerce between the two countries England would soon be heavily in debt." Together with Persia, India is the world's great treasury of design. Having decided upon the establishment of Schools of Art, it might then have been expected that educationists would have enquired upon what lines artistic education was given by these master draftsmen to their pupils and apprentices. This however, would have been running counter to the principle above enunciated: and so, in times gone by, the old fashioned South Kensington routine was introduced into India; for more advanced students, drawing from casts of Greek statuary and Gothic architecture, water colour sketching and all the rest of it, with the result, that quite a large number of men attained a second or third rate English standard. Probably no Indian artist so trained has done work good enough to be accepted by the Royal Academy, much less, good enough to be refused by that august body!

The true function of Schools of Art in India, is not to introduce European methods and ideals but to *gather up and revitalize the broken threads of Indian tradition,* to build up the idea of Indian art as an integral part of the national culture, and to relate the work of Indian craftsmen to the life and thought of the Indian people. So far from this, the School of Art craftsmen has hitherto worked essentially for a foreign public, making things which neither he nor his own people desired to *use,* but only to sell. No wonder the hinges do not work and the legs are wobbly. When Indian craftsmen worked for the Indian people they knew what was wanted, and why, and their work was altogether serviceable. Now that they work for tourists or occupy themselves in carving furniture for Anglo-Indian bungalows, or in making tea-pots overloaded with cheap ornament for Anglo-Indian tea-tables, it is naturally otherwise.

I have said that the true work of Schools of Art in India today, is to gather up and revitalise the broken threads of Indian traditions. But who can do this work? Not many Englishmen possess the necessary patience, or the necessary will. Like all true education in India, this work must be done by Indians. It is a question of national education. This question, touching as it does the vital base of the whole of Indian life, is of more importance than any political or economic reform. Rather than the achievement of any measure of progress in those directions, I would see Indians united in a demand for the *complete and entire control of Indian education in all its branches,* and determined that that education shall produce *Indian men and women*—not mere clerks, or makers of pretty curiosities for passing tourists.

To this end one thing is needful—that the present generation of 'educated' Indians should cease to be snobs. Mr. Burns perceives the true difficulty when he says that only a compelling movement from within the country could have accomplished the revival of Indian Art on traditional lines. That compelling movement lacked: and the result followed, that "India from an artistic point of view became and since remained a suburb of Paris and London, as she is the industrial suburb of Manchester and Birmingham."

The one great question today is this:—"Is the compelling movement within the country, which we call Nationalism, strong enough for the Herculean task before it, the conversion of a generation of parasites into a nation of orientals?" Every word of the answer to this question will be faithfully recorded in the progress or decline of Indian Art.

It rests with the Indian people themselves to say what the answer shall be.

# 6

## On the Study of Indian Art*

An art critic saturated with oriental traditions, when brought face to face with the remains of European art preserved in museums and galleries, will regard them in a different way from that in which we are accustomed to consider them. He will understand the drawing of Anglo-Saxon and mediaeval manuscripts and the painting of the early Italians or the Flemish primitives; he will understand the Gothic woodcut and the portraits of Holbein, and be sensitive to the beauty of the sculptures of Charters and of the mediaeval ivory Madonnas. But when he comes to examine modern works, he must be at a loss. He cannot understand them—he knows, of course, what they represent, but they convey no meaning to his mind, they have no burden which touches his heart. We, on the contrary, usually understand, or think we understand, only the modern works, which we admire in proportion to their fidelity in imitating the originals. If by chance we meet with any idealistic or imaginative work, if we are transported magically to some wonder-world of love or terror undescribed in history, unknown to the geographer, we are able without difficulty to preserve our souls from enthusiasm, by labelling all such art as 'decorative', and reserving the other name of 'fine art' for representations of things that we have already seen for ourselves. Fettered by such academic conventions, we approach light-heartedly the study of Indian art. It is not to be greatly wondered at that we

---

*A lecture to the Royal Asiatic Society, London, 1910.

often do not like it, and proceed from saying that it is not beautiful, to a further statement that it has no meaning.

But the fact that modern European art is mainly imitative, and so has no definite meaning of its own, ought not to blind us to the truth that taken as a whole, art is as much a means of expression, as much a language, as behaviour in general; both when sincere express the character and the preoccupations of the individual or race to which they belong. We are now accustomed to express thoughts and feelings mainly by means of spoken or written symbols. But a race of beings is quite easily conceivable, whose principal or only language should be another art, such as music, gesture, or painting, and there is no reason whatever every such language should not be at least as complex and full of resource for the expression of both concrete and abstract ideas as speech itself. There are some always amongst us for whom this is true: "to the true musician, music is more intelligible than speech... it is the art of thinking in sounds." Mendelsohn said that "any piece of music that he loved expressed thoughts not too indefinite to be put into words, but too definite." Mozart declared that he could not express his feelings and thoughts in poetry or painting, but that he could in music, for, "I am a musician."

In exactly the same way, for the plastic artist, painting or sculpture are languages by which he expresses and understands thoughts which are not in any sense vague, but which cannot be equally well, at least by him, expressed by means of words. "To give a clothing, a perfect form to one's thought, is to be an artist." It is immaterial whether the clothing be of words, or forms, or colours or sounds.

But just as the majority of persons do not understand more than the very elements of the language of music, so the majority do not understand more than the very elements of language of form and colour. Further, it is possible to understand a familiar dialect of such a language, and not to understand a dialect that is unfamiliar.

This last is the position of even the best qualified European writers upon Indian art.

How should the unfamiliar dialect be approached by one who proposes to interpret it to others? One method would be to examine the interpretation put upon its phrases by living or departed members of the same race, whose whole mental atmosphere and traditional culture are identical with or similar to those of the artists to be studied. The character of modern English education in India has, however, been such as to de-Indianize the minds of those who might otherwise have been able to comment in English upon Indian art as envisaged by a really Indian mind: and on the other hand, so far as I am aware, some extraordinary oversight has prevented any European writer from seeking assistance in Sanskrit writings on the theory of aesthetics, or even in a study of the Silpasastras. One would have supposed that these would have been made at least the foundation of a study of the theory and development of Indian art.

Failing these direct aids to the understanding of Indian art, which art, be it remembered, is essentially religious in content, —i.e., not necessarily dogmatic, but always concerned with reality— it would seem most natural to so study the life and thought of India, especially in its religious aspects, as to make it possible to see the world to some extent through Indian eyes, and so to gradually understand the expression of the Indian genius in Indian art.

In studying the art of any country, it is surely no more reasonable to ignore its meaning, which for creator and contemporary spectator was its most important quality, than it would be to consider the sound only, and not the meaning, in studying the work of any poet writing in an unknown language. Yet it is sometimes suggested that no qualification of knowledge of and sympathy for Indian mysticism and ideals of life and character is needed for the study of Indian art: that it is sufficient for the student, lacking these qualifications, to know only whether he 'likes' or 'dislikes' a given example of Brahmanical or Buddhist art: that such art has no connection with Indian idealistic thought, and that those who trace such a connection are themselves reading the Upanishads into the painting and sculptures.

Is not the opposite view more true, that the understanding of Indian art can only be attained through a realisation of the mental atmosphere in which it grew? One might illustrate from many European and Indian parallels. Take, for instance, the case of Gothic, an art closely related in spirit to Indian, and equally foreign to the modern temper. "To account for Gothic", writes Professor Lethaby in his book on 'Mediaeval Art', "we have to account for its historic basis and for the whole atmosphere of mysticism, chivalry and work-enthusiasm, with all the institutions, monastic, romantic and social, which formed its environment." A hundred years ago Gothic art was almost universally condemned as barbaric, in words very similar to those often applied to Indian art at the present day: it is possible now for authorities like the late Professor Middleton to write that in the thirteenth century, "it reached a higher pitch of perfection, aesthetic and technical, than has been obtained by any other country in the world." This may or may not be true: it may or may not also come to pass that Indian art of certain periods will be recognized as of supreme value; but it is certain that a new understanding of Indian art has somehow or other to be gained, and equally certain that this can only come through an understanding of the consciousness that finds expression in it. To take an Indian parallel: the late Professor G.U. Pope, in discussing his translation of the *Tiruvachagam,* says that his experience had taught him "that to get even a glimpse of the thought of a real poet, the student must often go down into the depths, must use every means to put himself in sympathy with his author, must learn to think and feel with him, and so it may be at last-come to understand him." It is the same with painting and sculpture, which are only other kinds of poetry; we must learn to think and feel as the artist thought and felt, if we would understand his art. If what he thought and felt repels, or even does not interest us, it follows that the interpretation of his art is not our real calling. No books are more completely valueless than those written about art by persons who lack emotional experience kindred to the artist's own. That is no reason why an European should not understand Indian art: for all great art deals with universal experiences, it is only that unfamiliarity of form sometimes blinds us to a real identity of passion. What is to be deplored is that books on Indian art have generally been written by persons who do not realise that art is an emotional experience at all. Leonardo di Vinci's illuminating phrase is an universal standard of criticism of works of art: "That drawing is best, which by its action best expresses the passion that animates the figure." This is of course applicable to any art whether music, painting or sculpture, if we understand drawing in a general sense of organised delineation. Its truth is self-evident and cuts away the ground from all criticism based on obvious external qualities of resemblance or so called perfection of form.

But what if you not only cannot feel, but openly regard it as superfluous to investigate, the passion that animates a work of art which you propose to study? One might well prefer the opposite extreme, and say with Blake, that "Enthusiastic admiration is the first principle of knowledge, and its last."

The function of the art critic and historian is after all a humble on: he is the servant of artists and his glory lies in perfection of service, and not in an exhibition of superior knowledge. His power too is limited; he can but lead those for whom he writes, to the waters of life,— he cannot make them drink. This they must do of their own free will, and this they can only do if they have suffered thirst. No pilgrim reaching a sacred spot desires the kind of information supplied in guide books: he wills to see the God, as we say in India, *dhulo payedarsan,* to worship with dusty feet. Worse than useless is the guide who takes his money and sends him empty away. Worse than useless, likewise, is the art critic whose sole concern is with dates and names and schools.

To take some concrete cases: the work of Professor Grünwedel (*Buddhist Art in India*), for all its mass of valuable facts, contains no attempt even at a constructive account of the 'nature of Indian,' nor any sign of an endeavour to explain the ideals and development of art that is distinctively Buddhist. Foucher's pre-occupation, again, with the details of European influence at a period when Europe had little to bestow in the way of artistic inspiration, would be comprehensible enough if the real character of the results were admitted. But when works of this kind are put forward as histories of *Indian art* they can only be described as futile and unscientific, if not as specious frauds. The same applies to the work of writers like Mr. Vincent Smith, who starts by saying that "after 300 A.D., Indian sculpture properly so-called hardly deserves to be reckoned as art." Those who write, and often with discernment and illumination, on archaeology or anthropology pure and simple, have no right to confuse issues by describing their books as works treating of art.

What then should be the aim of the writer of the history of the art of a given country or a given period? The prevailing idea indeed seem to be that that the proper thing to do is to enquire how far it, at any time, approximates to the art of some other country or period which the writer understands and approves of; to seek for and enlarge upon any traces of the influence of this approved style upon the style of the country or period investigated, and to condemn the remainder as barbaric. We are in fact reminded of the saying: "only works which are done in Italy can be called true painting, and therefore, we call good painting Italian."

Surely, the man who elects to describe and record the history of any art must set other and less banal aims than these before him. He must so put the matter before the student, that he is helped over initial difficulties of comprehension, and finally appreciates the unknown art better than he did before; otherwise what end is served by writing or by reading what is written? I think there is not one quite great enough to say that this or that art is highest or best, and another second or third: nor is the art critic or historian called upon to deliver any judgment, of this kind. He needs only to be able to recognize truth and life when he sees them. All good art has similar qualities, and so also, all bad art is bad in much the same way. But every great cycle of artistic expression has certain characteristics and a particular genius of its own, and expresses certain preoccupations. If the critic's work is to be of any value he must so understand this genius as to be able to trace the evolution of its expression, to define the period of its fullest development, to point to the examples in which its bias is most perfectly expressed, and above all to correlate its form with the movement of the human spirit that finds expression through it.

The conviction is sometimes forced upon the student, that European writers on Indian art have been, what in Mr. Vincent Smith's opinion, the inhabitants of Hindustan have always been, "singularly indifferent to aesthetic merit, and little qualified to distinguish between good and bad art." The convincing proof of this is to be found in the illustrations, varying in degree of inadequacy, which disgrace the pages of English, French and German handbooks to Indian art. The matter is well put by Gustave be Bon, (quoted by Maindron, himself one of the worst offenders!):

"It is not from the cuts or bad lithographs which appear in certain works on Hindu mythology that one can form any idea of the sculpture. It really seems as if the authors of these works had made a point of selecting the most wretched examples. It is owing to these unfortunate reproductions that there has been formed the opinion now prevalent in Europe, that Hindu sculpture is a quite, inferior art."

We should know what to think of an oriental art critic who judged all European art on the basis of a collection of tradesmen's oleographs, and modern Roman Catholic plaster saints, or, still worse, from the standpoint of religious prejudice. This is however, practically, what European writers have done with Indian art. As the French writer already mentioned remarks, Hindu art "has been judged by most writers with injustice, for which the only excuse appears to be its extraordinary naivete, when it is not the result of a pious bigotry as exaggerated as that of the conquering Musulmans."

The Indian collections to be seen in European museums, especially in London, are open to similar criticism. Their miscellaneous contents never seem to be determined by expert selection.

It is perfectly useless to approach an art like Indian, armed with conventional ideas about idolatry, superstition, polytheism, priestcraft, and the like. All these things flourished exceedingly in the noblest centuries of Christian art. Every time and place has its own illusions and superstitions. The modern superstition is the superstition of facts, which is a very much more dangerous thing than any superstition of the imagination. The extremely materialistic character of most European religious thought since the Reformation has made it almost impossible for European writers to interpret the art of a people who regard a belief in the reality of phenomena as in itself the worst sort of superstition. Since the Renaissance moreover, all ideas of 'Gods' have been coloured by the patriarchal types of the

Greek Olympus; it is only just beginning to be realised that these 'beautiful humanities' were not in any profound sense religious conceptions; the true Greek religion (which was gradually overwhelmed by materialistic thought) was something quite different, more passionate, mystic, remote and very much more like the religions of the East. The Indian Gods have so far been studied by missionaries and anthropologists, instead of by philosophers and artists. But it is only when students of Indian art understand exactly what the idea of a God, or any particular God, stands for in the Indian mind and heart, that a sane criticism of Indian art can be made. The mythologies so far written are useless from this point of view.

Perhaps the greatest obstacle to the scientific study of Indian art lies in the modern conception of art as essentially imitative, and that general confusion of the aims of science and art which is exemplified in 'photographic criticism'. Oriental art as a whole does not aim at the reproduction of the facts of nature, objectively considered; its aim is suggestion, selection, emphasis, design—the representation, not of objective but of subjective fact. It is therefore perfectly futile to complain that Indian does not represent the so-called facts of nature : it expresses the realities of life, and it would mould the facts of nature nearer to the heart's desire. The greatest art is creative and living; it is in its faithfulness to this ideal that there lies the significance of Oriental art for Western students as a recent writer and critic remarks. The greatest practical value of Eastern art for us lies in the fact "that those essential principles, which in our thirst for verisimilitude, we have overlaid, have been upheld with far greater constancy by the artists of the East."

It is a tragic thing, however, that in spite of all difficulties, some Western minds in modern times have understood Indian art, and been more deeply moved by it, than any Indian. Not one of us in all the nineteenth century thought of writing any book on Indian art, even as good as those European books that I have criticised. Even today it is far easier to lecture to an ordinary European audience on Indian art, and find some understanding of it, than it is to secure this understanding from an Indian audience. In all other civilised countries while the general public remains indifferent to good art, there are small groups of persons who can feel the passion of, and care for any good art. In India, not only is the good part of Indian art quite ignored, but 'educated' men are capable of understanding only the commonest academic art of Europe, and care nothing for the real masters of painting and sculpture. What a commentary on the worthlessness of a century of so-called 'English education'!

Suppose that at first we, whether European or Indian, do not understand or care for Indian art: let us at least avoid the thought that it is given to us alone to know what are beauty and truth. We must realise that other men besides ourselves have sought their images, and sought them not as we now seek, outside ourselves, but in their own hearts. These men lived in a world which we now know less than the Antarctic or the frozen north: a world perhaps more real, more wonderful than ours, certainly quite different. Only because we do not know it have we called it unreal: but until we know it as we know our own how may we say whether or no they painted images of truth? At least we should give thanks to them for showing to us that our world is no absolute *Ding an sich*, and that the shadows of reality are of many varied outlines and move across our vision with mysterious elusiveness. Perhaps the greatest end of any art is to show to us that no one shadow is eternal or self-existent, only Light is that.

# 7

# Facial Expression in Indian Sculpture

To understand the ideal of expression aimed at in Indian religious sculpture, we need to understand the ultimate Indian ideal of character. In Buddhism, the 'Ten fetters that bind a traveller on the path, and have to be overcome before Nirvana is attainable are the illusion of self-consciousness, doubt, trust in rites and ceremonies, hatred, love of life, longing after heaven, self-righteousness, and ignorance.' The similar Hindu ideal is described in many places, e.g., *Bhagavadgita*, XII, 12-19:—"Hateless toward all born beings, void of the thought of an I and a my, bearing indifferently pain and pleasure, before whom the world is not dismayed and who is not dismayed before the world, who is void of joy, impatience, fear, dismay, who is desireless, pure, adept, impartial, who rejoices not, hates not, grieves not, desires not, who renounces alike fair and foul, who is indifferent alike to foe and friend, in honour and dishonour, in heat and in cold, in joy and in pain, free of attachment."

Such is the character predicated of him who is fit for Nirvana, the Jivanmukta, he who is "dear to Me". Perfection in the same sense must also be the character of a Buddha or an Ishvara, for it is only by self-conquest that the status of a god is ever attained.

The whole ideal might be summed up in the words of Eckhardt: "Real sanctification consists in this, that the spirit remains immovable and unaffected by all import of love or hate, joy, or sorrow, honor or shame, as a huge mountain is unstirred by a gentle breeze. This immovable sanctification

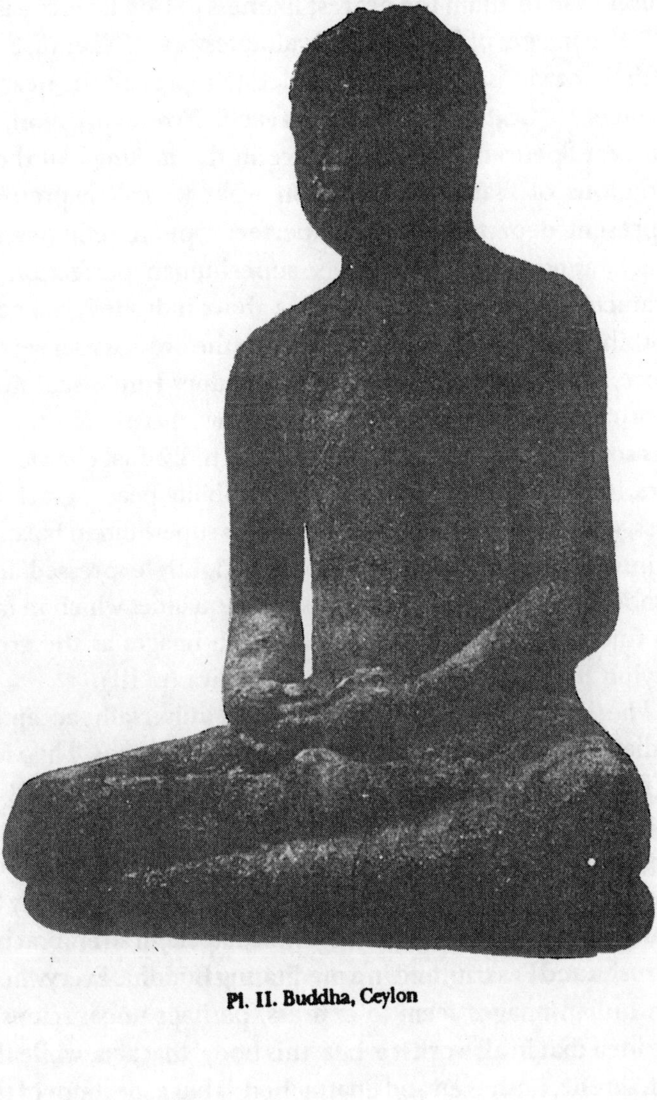

Pl. II. Buddha, Ceylon

causes man to attain the nearest likeness to God he is capable of." The images of Buddha, of Avalokitesvara, of Vishnu, Siva, in their sattvic aspects were intended to represent the nearest likeness to God that art could reach. Now expression, as Herbert Spencer puts it, is feature in the making. All those variations of feature constitution what we call expression represent departures, from a perfect type. A religious art which aims at representing a superhuman perfection of character, equanimity, in the sense above indicated, can have nothing to do with facial expression in the ordinary sense; the more, 'human' in expression, the less does Hindu sculpture approach its own perfection. That is to say, there is no room in this sort of art for the representation of individual characteristics, for portraiture. Such qualities as nobility, peace, graciousness, which involve in their perfection a superhuman balance of intellect and emotion, can alone be rightly 'expressed' in a symbol (idol) of Divine Life. It is these qualities which in fact do find expression in the faces of such images as the great Ceylon Buddha, pl. II, or the Tanjore Siva (pl.III).

The ideal which informs the most universally accepted Indian Gospel, is that of action without attachment. This view of life, thus expressed in words, is equally clearly stated in sculpture or painting representing human or divine beings engaged in strenuous action, but having at the same time upon the face an expression of unshaken peace. The peace may be equally expressed in a destroying Dharmapala, in an embracing Purusha and Prakriti, and in a meditating Buddha. Everywhere the Indian images seem to express, perhaps unconsciously, the idea that in all work it is but 'this body' that acts, while the self, serene, unshaken and unattached, is but a spectator of the drama where itself is manifested as an actor.

Even the divine ideal has its basis in humanity: one may see today everywhere surviving in India the mountainous, silent human forms, the features immovably composed, and the

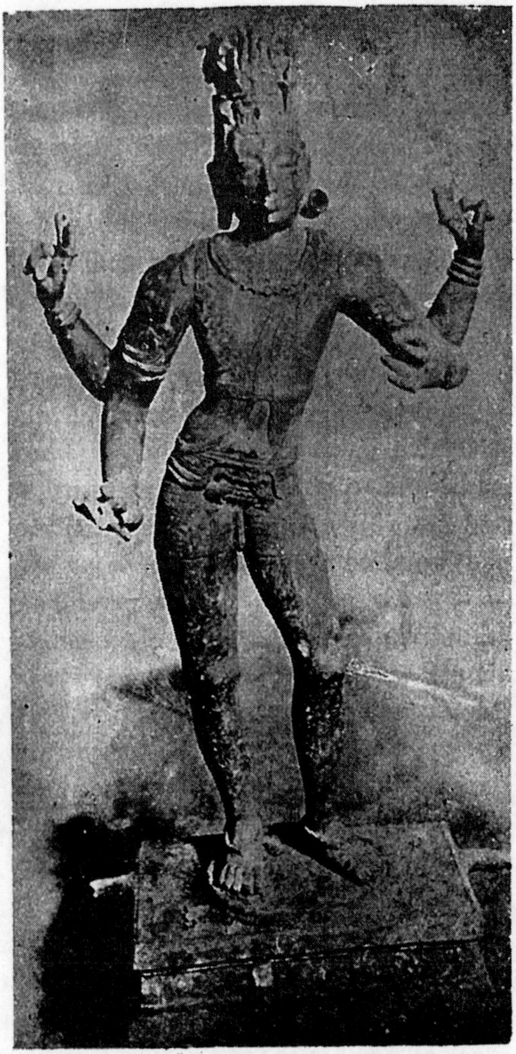

Pl. III. Siva, Tanjore

indescribable stillness which belongs to Indian sculpture: one may see on the ghats of any tirtham the lion waist and slender limbs of types that might otherwise seem to have been carefully exaggerated by the artist: and as Lafcardio Hearn so beautifully tells us, the gentle mysterious smile of so many Buddhist images is the very same that is natural to peoples for whom the subjective life is very real. These significant things emphasised by art, have grown into an ideal and a tradition which have reacted powerfully on life itself, and find expression almost as much in images of saints or kings as in the figures of gods. The divine ideal gives to these a certain strange and beautiful impersonality that makes them like the gods whose servants, or, as some would say, incarnate selves they partly were. Yet in the face and gesture of a figure like the Ceylon Sundaramurti Swami (pl. IV) we find a real humanity: he is a boy, and not a god. If we contrast this with the strange un-humanness of expression, the remoteness and repose of contemporary figures of Siva himself, we shall realise that it was not because the Indian sculptor could not represent character, but because we have not always understood the kind of character that he wished to represent, that his work has seemed monstrous and expressionless.

In another way, moreover, Indian sculpture is extraordinarily expressive. This is in its representation of gesture. "A good painter," says Leonardo, "has two chief objects to paint, namely, man, and the intention of his soul. The first is easy, and the second difficult, because he has to represent it through the attitudes and movements of the limbs." It is here that Indian sculpture excels all other in the world. Even Egyptian though it has the wonderful stillness, has not the impassioned movement of Indian. In such an image as the Sundaramurti Swami from Ceylon, there is a sense of breathless eagerness and rapturous surprise that give it a quite peculiar beauty; equally impressive are the passion of repose in a Dhyani

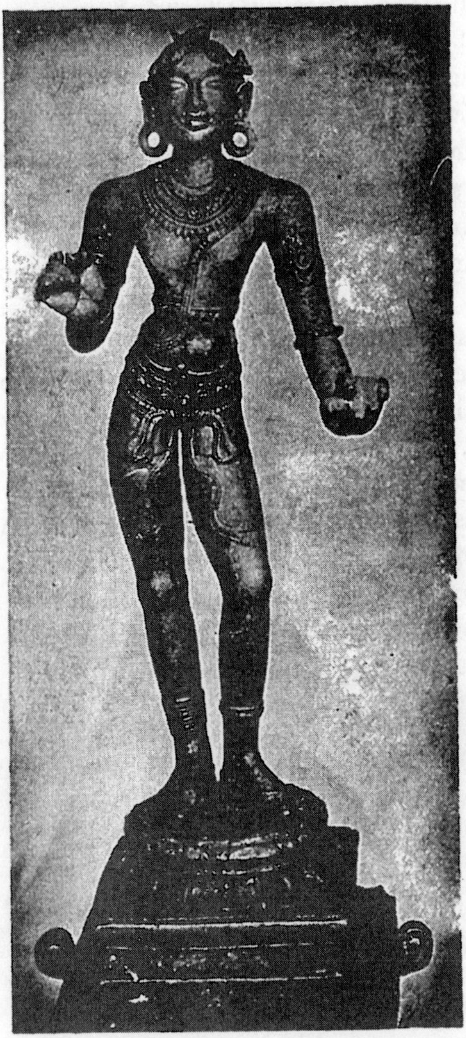

Pl. IV. Sundaramurti Swami, Ceylon

Buddha, and the sense of whirlwind movement in a Dharmapala. In Europe we are too apt to think of human beings as faces only, and to think of the body as a mere accessory. Even the hands we do not notice. But for the sculptor a man is not a face: he is like a mountain or a cathedral, a single unity of which the face is only a part.

This essentially sculpturesque quality is everywhere conspicuous in Indian art. Perhaps it may serve as a compensation to those who regret a lack of humanism in the Indian ideal of facial expression. In any case, whether we demand of art merely the reflection of ourselves, or the vision of something beyond us, it is certain that we must understand and recognise, if not accept, the Indian (Hindu or Buddhist) ideal of character, and we must know something of the extent to which this character has been actually realised in life. The complaint of lack of expression in Indian art is due either to lack of acquaintance with the finest work, or of a failure to comprehend the kind of expression arrived at.

# 8

## On Mughal and Rajput Painting*

After the first great period of Indian painting, of which the painted chaityas at Ajanta are witness still, we have to face an almost entire absence of actual remains, until we reach the middle of the sixteenth century. We know, of course, from literary references and other indications, that the art was continuous. But no mediaeval wall paintings are preserved, though a few Buddhist painted book covers are found.

It may be remarked that there are three reasonable ways of using painting, other than the merely decorative ornamentation of the smaller articles of industrial or cultural value. The noblest of these ways is that art of wall painting in which the Italians and the Ajanta artists alike excelled. There is then the Japanese method of painting pictures on cloth, pictures that are carefully put away, and only taken out one by one and hung singly in a room, otherwise almost bare of furniture or decoration: the room is filled by, and dominated by a single picture, which the spectator can appreciate without distraction or disturbance. Thirdly we have portfolio paintings, which form a unity in themselves apart from any direct relation to an architectural environment.

To this last class belong most of the Indian paintings (with a few exceptions of paintings on the walls of palaces) of the sixteenth, seventeenth and eighteenth centuries. There are also various book illustrations, illuminations, but this is more characteristic of Persian than of Indian art. The Indian port-

* Originally delivered as a lecture to the Indian Society of Oriental Art, Calcutta, 1910.

folio paintings are not to be dismissed as decorative art: indeed, inasmuch as they are entirely independent of environment, no kind of painting could be less accurately defined as 'decorative' in a depreciatory sense. They are most varied in treatment and the range of subject matter is equally great. They reflect both the life and the ideals of men with extraordinary intimacy,—the actual and the dream-world of two great Oriental cultures at the most dramatic moment of their contact.

Indian portfolio pictures are not a branch of Persian art nor an importation of the Mughals. Only certain elements in this art are Persian and Mughal (i.e., Turki or Mongolian). Persian art is essentially one of book illustrations in which brilliant colours and much gold are used. It has small variety of content. Fighting, drinking and flirtation are the usual motifs. Other elements—such as portraiture (where it occurs)— are due, as in India, to Timurid (Mughal) influence. Persian painting is pretty, even beautiful, it is graceful, lyrical, exquisite in colouring and design, but it is never passionate. It tells us of magnificent adventures and of scented gardens, not of the love of God or the infinite joy and sorrow of the loves of women or men. It does not reveal to us the character of men or the souls of animals and trees and mountains. Its types are conventional rather than ideal, and one wearies of the languid mannerism, notwithstanding its marvellous charm.

The Indian art is essentially one of picture paintings. Book illustrations are few, and with some exceptions, unimportant. There is immense variety and depth of content, humanistic and religious. The pictures fall into two groups, Rajput and Mughal: I shall speak of the latter first.

The term Indo-Persian should now be definitely reserved for certain work, (of whatever date, but mostly early, i.e., about 1550-1610) in which there is a real mixture of two styles: an almost equivalent term would be early Mughal, i.e., work done under Mughal patronage up to the earlier part of the reign of

Jehangir. This Indo-Persian painting includes: (a) Indian copies of the illustrations to Persian epics, usually decidedly inferior to the originals, (b) Illuminations in a somewhat similar style illustrating Persian translations of Hindu books such as the *Ramayana, Yoga Vashishta, Kalilah* and *Dimnah (Anwar Soheli)* and *Suz-u-Gudaz*. These are often of the highest interest and have really great qualities: the landscape however remains quite artificial, (c) separate pictures, in a style similar to (b), illustrating Persian romances such as Laila-Majnun: and, (d) portraits with a combination of Persian and Indian characteristics.

This represents the earlier stage of Mughal art in India. The true Mughal style in India belongs to the seventeenth century*— before that, it is developing: after, it is declining. In the seventeenth century the vigorous Central Asian (i.e., Mongol or Timurid) influence predominates over the more effeminate Persian element and both combine with the art of the country itself to form a self-complete and exquisite new art which attains its zenith in the reigns of Jahangir and Shah Jahan.

This art is secular and dramatic in its content, excelling most in portraiture. Its outlook is essentially upon the present moment, it is deeply interested in the doings of aristocratic men—it is not an idealisation of life, but a representation of it. In other words, the most characteristic features of Mughal painting are its profound interest in individual character, its analytic rather than synthetic method and its concern with the doings of kings and courtiers, rather than with the visions of saints or the lyric symbolism of an agricultural race.

The Mughal style of painting, though built up with the materials of many different traditions, is most undeniably

---

*The best Mughal work of the 16th century is the most Persian, of the 17th century, the most Indian.

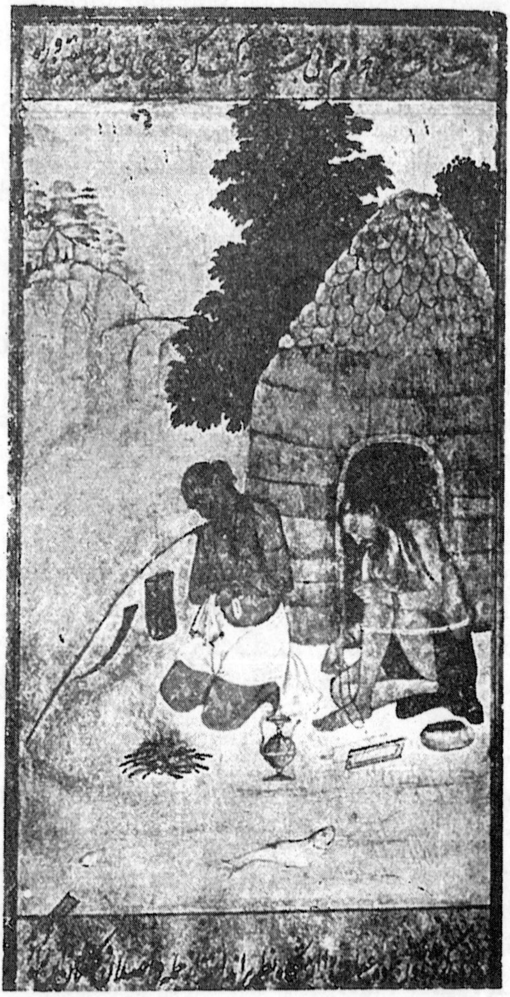

Pl. V. Yogis: Illustration to Persian translation of the Yoga Vashishta

original, in the same sense that the Mughal culture in India is as a whole original. It is true that it combines Persian, Indian and other elements: but out of these it creates something new. The mind of the age, essentially synthetic, and not merely eclectic, finds its truest expression in the character of such a man as Akbar. This type of cultivated mind, now only too rare, nourished alike by the streams of Persian and Indian religious thought, romance, and art, is as truly original as can well be looked for. In Akbar it was combined with great personal genius, which found full expression, because it was not opposed to the spirit of his age, but embodied in itself the highest ideals and more or less unconscious tendencies of that age, developed to their fullest extent.

It is the same with Mughal architecture—it is a new architecture which combines two completely different styles to produce what has been called an improved third style;[1] 'entirely original'.[2]

At the same time it must be recognized that the true Mughal painting was not fully evolved in the time of Akbar himself. He was not perhaps a very good judge of art. At any rate very few of his own painters produced work of real importance, because they were too much employed in imitating Persian mannerisms. But this condition did not last—after 1600, the new style disengages itself from these restrictions with extreme rapidity.

The Mughal schools of painting in India cover a period of barely two centuries, during which the art grows up, flourishes and declines. Unlike the Rajput styles, it owes very much to foreign sources. The most important of these foreign elements is that of the schools of Turkistan (Bokhara and

[1]A. Muller, *Der Islam in Morgen and Abendland*, II, p. 386.
[2]Von Garbe, *Akbar, Emperor of India*, p. 25.

Samarqand), the home of the Timurids, who became the "Great Mughals" of India. These Timurids were great patrons of literature and art. In Babar's memoirs we find in the midst of accounts of adventures and campaigns, delightfully simple references to flowers and painters. Akbar's patronage of painters is too well known to need description here. But of all these kings Shah Jahan was the greatest artist. He himself was an expert calligrapher: and in his reign or just before Mughal painting and architecture reached their zenith, and exhibited that combination of grandeur with feminine elegance of detail, which characterises, for example, the great Fort at Agra.

Akbar seems at first to have employed a number of Hindu artists to copy illuminated pictures in the Persian *Shah Namahs* and similar works. These book illustrations, in what may be called the bastard Persian style, have singularly little interest, or value. We find however, by the close of Akbar's reign, a truly 'mixed,' school in existence, which though it soon gave place to a more completely Indian style, produced some exceedingly beautiful and interesting works. The Persian influence appears in the scenery and in some details of the drawing and also in the fact that this Indo-Persian or early Mughal art is mainly one of book illustration.

Certain Indian books (such as the *Yoga Vashishta)* translated into Persian for the benefit of Akbar himself and others like him unfamiliar with Sanskrit gave to the Indian painters the opportunity for self-expression which the imitation of Persian pictures denied to them. In such books we find illustrations wholly Hindu in sentiment and subject matter, and exceedingly accomplished in execution, although the landscape is altogether artificial (pl. V).

Portraiture, however, is the essentially Mughal contribution to Indian art, though it is not wholly unknown to the painters of the Rajput schools. This factor is rather due to Central Asian than to Persian influence. In Central Asian art, Chinese influence is very marked, and it is interesting to reflect that the debt which China owed to India from so long ago, for her Buddhist art, she partly repaid through the hands of the later Mughal ('Monghol') invaders.

The Mughals themselves originated near Samarqand in Turkistan where a remarkable school of draughtsmanship, largely based on Chinese tradition, had long flourished. Its characteristics are exemplified in the magnificent portrait of Tamerlane in the Bodleian and by such drawings as the 'Running Warrior,' in the collection of Mr. Golonbeff. Communication between Samarqand and India was long maintained, and we cannot doubt that, as Mr. Migeon remarks, 'the Moguls of Delhi continued to import those gaily illuminated books from Turkistan.' Moreover we have, in some signed portraits preserved in the British Museum, definite proof that artists from Turkistan worked at the Mughal Courts in India in the seventeenth century. A number of these are the work of 'Muhammad Nadir of Samarqand'.

It was, I believe, this art which gave the characteristic impulse to portraiture, to Mughal art in India. This was no small matter, for, as Mr. Vincent Smith, remarks, India possesses, for the period of two centuries under consideration, a gallery of historical portraits such as no other country in the world can show. It would be difficult to exaggerate the exquisite perfection of draughtsmanship of these. As Mr. Binyon says, "How beautiful some of these portraits are! What a world of experience or of youthful romance is in these delicately outlined heads!"

The Bodleian 'Portrait of a Dying Man' (pl. VI) marks the highest level of achievement of Mughal painting. In this picture, with its burden of most intense feeling, there is no touch of sentimentality: we perceive the naked soul of a man, face to face with death, already forgetful of the body and intent on things that are real. Here is typically embodied the

Mussalman reverence for humanity, and humanism attains an intensity of expression which can only be called religious. Here, indeed, Mughal painting rises above its usual secularity of content to a level of grandeur not lower than that of the idealism of any more strictly religious art. Such paintings are rare and very precious.

With the advent of Aurangzeb, puritanical, indifferent to art, and representative of the first decline of the Mughal genius, the art also begins to decay, although very splendid works continued to be produced so late as the earliest part of the eighteenth century. After this it rapidly loses its qualities of spontaneity, distinction and refinement. In its later days the Nawabs of Oudh were its principal patrons, and it is now only represented by the Delhi trade in ivory miniatures and some lingering influence on a bastard school of European portrait painting in oils.

Very different in character is Rajput painting, that Hindu art which as Abul Fazl himself said, 'surpasses our conception of things'. It has a range of content and a depth of passion foreign to the sentimental Persian idylls and battle and hunting scenes, and rarely touched in the Mughal studies of individual character. All the self-restraint and the abandonment, the purity and wild extravagance, the tenderness and fury of Hinduism find expression here. The art is religious, lyrical, and epic. It has many of the qualities of folk-song and ballad. Portraiture is comparatively rare. It is an art more deeply rooted in the national life, than the courtly secular art of the Mughals, for all its exquisite beauty and refinement, ever was or could have been. For the Mughal courtier, life was a glorious pageant: for the Rajput and the Brahman, life was an eternal sacrament.

The Rajput painting is the descendant of that art of tempera painting which we lose sight of at Ajanta; and of the mediaeval work of which so little trace remains, though we cannot doubt

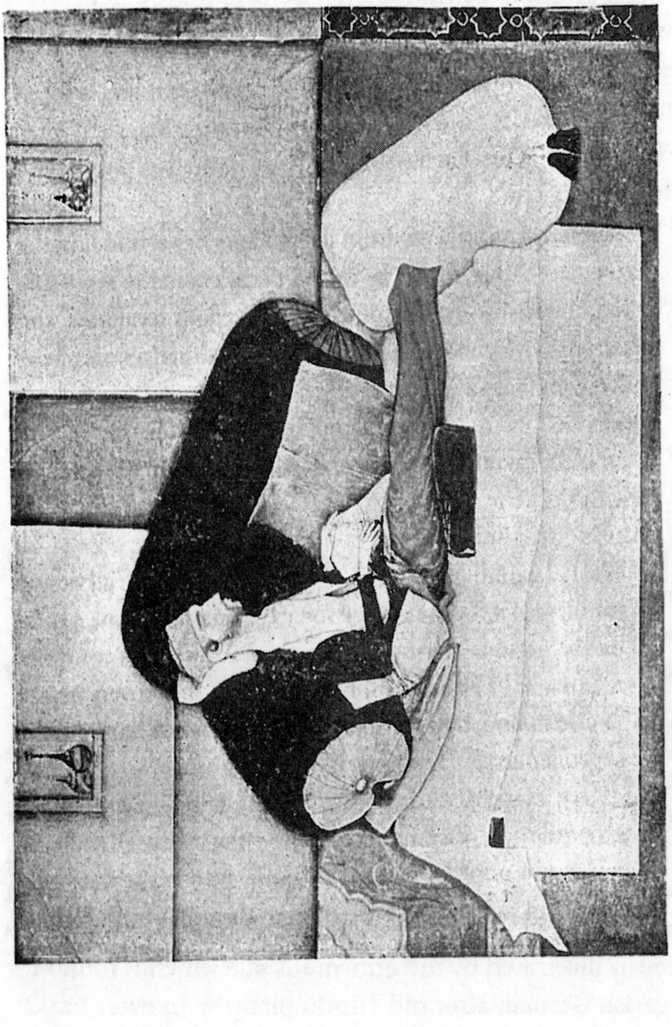

Pl. VI. The Dying Man: Mughal Miniature in the Bodleian, Oxford

that the art existed continuously. It is still to some extent an art of painting on walls, and even the portfolio paintings bear clear traces of their mural ancestry. Persian painting belongs to the pages of books: but Indian painting even when small belongs to an art that has stepped from the walls of palaces and temples.

Rajput painting is an art in its old age. As we find it in the sixteenth century, it may be called decadent in the sense that it has obviously—in spite of a still marvellous loveliness, and the scarcely surpassable perfection of occasional masterpieces fallen away from a greater level of achievement. It is a folk-art descended from a more magnificent tradition. Those who possess the faculty of imaginative reconstruction will catch in this folk-art the accents of a loftier speech than that of its intrinsic achievement.

Mughal painting on the contrary is an art in the full vigour of youth, with infinite courage for experiment and the conditions for almost over-rapid evolution. Whereas the whole development of Hindu and Buddhist painting covers nearly two millenniums, that of Mughal painting covers hardly more than two centuries. Hence it is that Mughal work is easy to date, for the styles succeed each other rapidly. It is often difficult to estimate the date of a Rajput painting—the style itself is almost constant and some bad work was done even in the sixteenth century, and some good work even in the nineteenth. Rajput painting indeed is scarcely yet extinct. Its popular character is curiously illustrated by the enormous sale which is found for the garish German after old Hindu pictures, in every bazaar.

The Rajput paintings are specially serious, epic and romantic. They often express a profound sense of sympathy for all natural life and a sense of the fundamental unity of all created things. The religious symbolism is sometimes mythological, sometimes humanistic. The types are ideal rather than conventional.

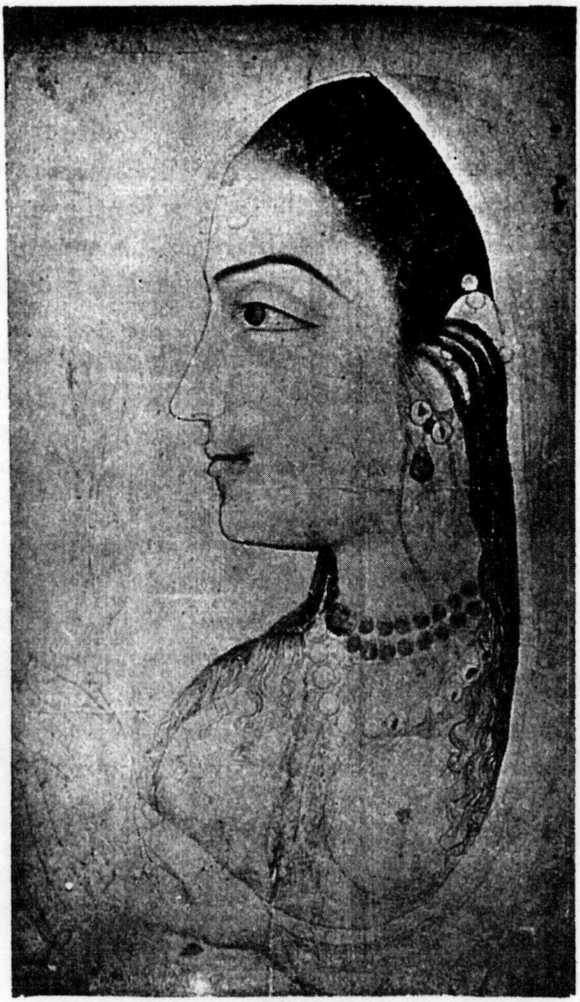

Pl. VII. Rajput drawing from Jaipur, Bodleian, Oxford

The Rajput paintings geographically considered, fall into two related groups, the Himalayan (or 'Pahari') schools and the schools of Rajputana. The Hindu painting of southern India is of a different character: it may fairly be called decadent and is almost exclusively mythological. The Himalayan style is most typically represented by the peculiar Kangra valley type, those of the plains by the artists of Jaipur. It is, at least, in the Kangra valley and Jaipur that the old traditions have longest survived.

The strength of the Kangra school lies in the Vaishnava paintings, with their burden of love and their lyric humanistic symbolism. They tell of Rama's wandering in the forest: we see Him with Sita, guarded by Lakshmana. We see the bears and monkeys building Rama's bridge and storming the citadel of Lanka, and these things live for us as never before, because we are made not merely aware of them but made to feel them. The pictures reveal to us the life of Krishna as a child, as a boy and as hero. All love human and divine (for India these are one and the same) are told of in the herd-girls' adoration of him. This Vaishnava art is an idealisation of love in every phase of its expression, a very consecration of humanity. Animals are in the bond; and as it is written in the *Ramayana*, the trees themselves bend towards the Lord as He passes.

The Kangra drawings excel in the representation of movement and expressive gesture. The painters were 'curious of certain movements of tenderness and ardour' of which their expression is most passionate. The meeting of eyes, the locking of hand in hand, the grace and shyness of women, their adoration for men, the abandoned sadness of desertion or vain desire are rendered with exquisite purity of sentiment. Again, the hosts of heaven are led by Durga against the powers of evil—she is old and ugly and sword in hand rides on a lion, breathing flames that consume the asuras; or a naked woman on an open plain she is the guru of an assembly of sages; or as an exquisite young girl, as Parvati, she sits by Siva, stringing for him the heads of a thousand Brahmas as a garland (for she is the destroyer of Time).

Nor does the value of this art depend solely on its subject matter—its wonderful idealisation of pastoral life or its daring contrast of the forces of good and evil, denial and desire—or upon the fact that it speaks a language of the folk, the mother tongue of all those who love the Bhagavata, the Adorable. For the way in which these things are told of is nearly always intrinsically lovely, or powerful, or amusing. Its productions range in manner from extreme refinement to extreme crudity; but they are never vulgar and very rarely without interest. Some of the purely mythological work however has little in it but a sort of rather arid symbolism, not beautifully expressed.

The pictures of the Jaipur school are somewhat harder and less accomplished than those of Kangra. But amongst them are some of exquisite perfection. Of the *ragas* and *raginis,* personified musical modes, there are particularly fine examples. There is also some admirable animal drawing, and a certain amount of portraiture. Moreover the Jaipur school has special interest on account of the large scale of some of the work, and because much of it is still to be found in situ on the walls of palaces, as at Udaipur and Bikaner. At Jaipur there are wonderfully beautiful large pictures of Radha and Krishna, with groups of girl musicians whose remote grace reminds us irresistibly of Botticelli.

In painting of the Jaipur school, in Rajputana, there is an unmistakable though very intermittent Chinese element. This element is of a different character from that which enters into Mughal and Persian art, and appears to be more direct. It is conspicuous in such treatment of scenery as we find represented on the walls of the island palace at Udaipur, and the old palace at Bikaner. There seems to have long been direct intercourse by sea between Gujarat and China, and even at the present day there continues a trade in embroidery specially designed for the Indian market.

An important factor in Rajput painting is the survival in it of features directly traceable to the older Buddhist art from which it is ultimately descended. Amongst these may be mentioned the composition of a *parinirvana*, in pictures of the death of Bhishma; the spiral convention for water: the constant use of lotus lakes and lotus flowers: and the tender feeling for birds and animals.

Amongst other rather characteristic features may be mentioned the fact that the scenery is characteristically Indian: the low hills of Rajputana and the white peaks of the Himalayas are constantly represented. Persian influence when present is always apparent in the artificiality of the landscape—ultimately derivable from the Chinese mountain convention. The trees represented are always Indian, most often the mango. We never meet with the flowering shrubs and wind blown cypress of Persian art. The larger trees are often, especially in Kangra work, wreathed with flowering *lianes*. The angular margins of lakes and ponds are very characteristic: we do not find those little streams meandering through flowery meadows that adorn the pages of Persian books. The costume of men and women is almost purely Indian. There can be no doubt that foreign influence on costume and architecture was extensive and early: but this does not of course make the style of drawing foreign in any sense. The 3-pointed crown, each point with a ball, is a very characteristic Hindu element; and the *dupata* and bodice (with bare waist) used by women. Of subject-matter I have already spoken. In Mughal work of the seventeenth century there is not a little contemporary Italian influence. But if we consider the Indian work as a whole, especially Rajput, what most impresses us is its kinship with earlier, pre-Raphaelite Italian painting. We are constantly reminded of Giotto, Benozzo Gozzoli, Botticelli, Francesco Francia and the

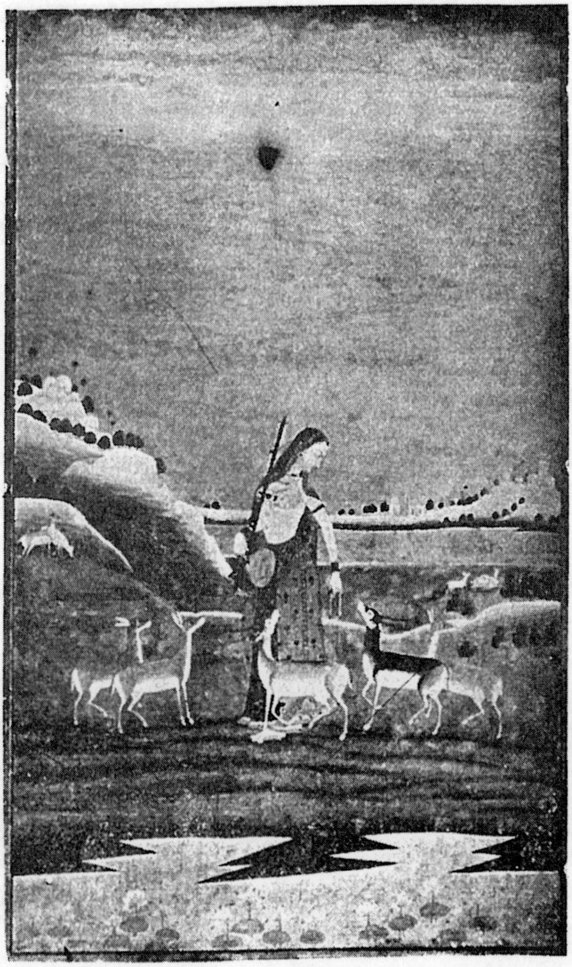

Pl. VIII. Ragini Tori: Rajput picture from Jaipur

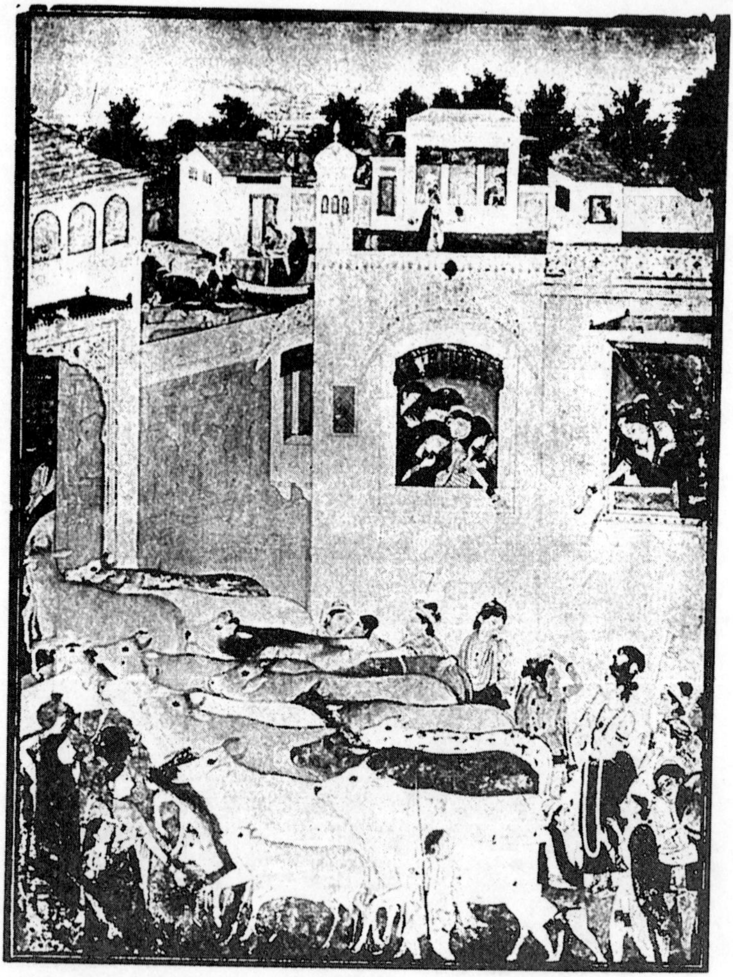

Pl. IX. The Divine Cowherd: Rajput picture from Kangra

earlier Italian wood-cutters. We find expressed in both arts the same childlike purity of soul, the same gentle wonder at the beauty of flowers and animals, the same mysterious sweet serenity in the faces of women, the same worship of humanity as a symbol of the divine. And this is due not to borrowing, but to similarity of impulse. For the human spirit is not so constructed that it can borrow a nobility of expression without possessing that nobility within itself.

For all its charm, however, this art has definite limitations. It is no longer developing and as has been already pointed out, often needs some faculty of imaginative reconstruction in the spectator. It can have no appeal to those who are not attuned to its spirit of devotion and tenderness, or cannot accept its magnificent but uncompromising conventions. It is essentially true to human nature, but it makes no pretence to realism. It is the exact counterpart of the contemporary Indian poetry, and this is as it should be, for all true painting is a sort of poetry. It belongs to a time when the fantastic notion of representation as the highest aim of art had not been imagined in the East: it is purely expressive, and whether great or humble, it keeps its hold for ever on those who have ever felt its spell and who find in it the only visible record of a world of wonder and beauty that is passing away before our very eyes, unrecognized and unregretted.

Such are the chief characteristics of painting of the Rajput school. If it is ever possible to write in full the history of painting in India it is this art of the country itself, which, after Ajanta, must form its main theme. Compared with the significance of this religious art, so romantic and impassioned, even, in some respects more brilliant, achievements of the Persian, Central Asian and Indian painters at the Mughal courts must be treated as an episode.

The Mughal painting, however, showed that it was still possible to found a new art on the basis of the old traditions:

foreign influences were, not perhaps easily, but at last effectually, assimilated, and the result was a new and great art, which, as I have tried to show, is truly original. Perhaps this possibility of assimilating foreign influences and creating a new art in which traditional elements still on the whole predominate may be taken as a hopeful sign for the future development of Indian painting. It is already along these lines that the latest movement tends.

# 9

## Night Effects in Indian Pictures

The representation of night effects is a very characteristic feature of Indian painting. It is true that in Persian illuminations we occasionally find night scenes depicted, when necessary to the illustration of the subject in hand, but in such paintings there is not representation of night effects: we gather only from the burning cressets and lighted candles that events are taking place at night. In Indian paintings we have all the romance and mystery of night itself, painted for its own sake. The night in India, almost more than the day, is the time of awakeness and of action; it is the time for discourse and entertainment, for travel, for worship and for love. It is a time of exquisite contrasts, when the torch of a guide or the flame of a camp fire lights up the traveller's face, or the crowded candles illuminate the gold-inwoven dress and tinkling jewels of the dancer. At night the water-fete is at its height, and one may see the gaily decorated barge of a great guild of craftsmen, or of a prince or Rajah, threading its way amongst the mass of smaller craft that crowd round the boats where music and dancing are going on, or provisions are for sale. At night the lover waits for her beloved. At night the gods are borne in procession round the temple ambulatory, with music and dance. And it is at night that men and women steal away to lonely hermitages to talk with those for whom the world is vanity, or go with offerings and devotion to some forest shrine of Mahadev. All this full life finds passionate expression in Indian painting.

The four pictures which illustrate the subject of this chapter need little explanation. The first, 'Riding at Night' represents,

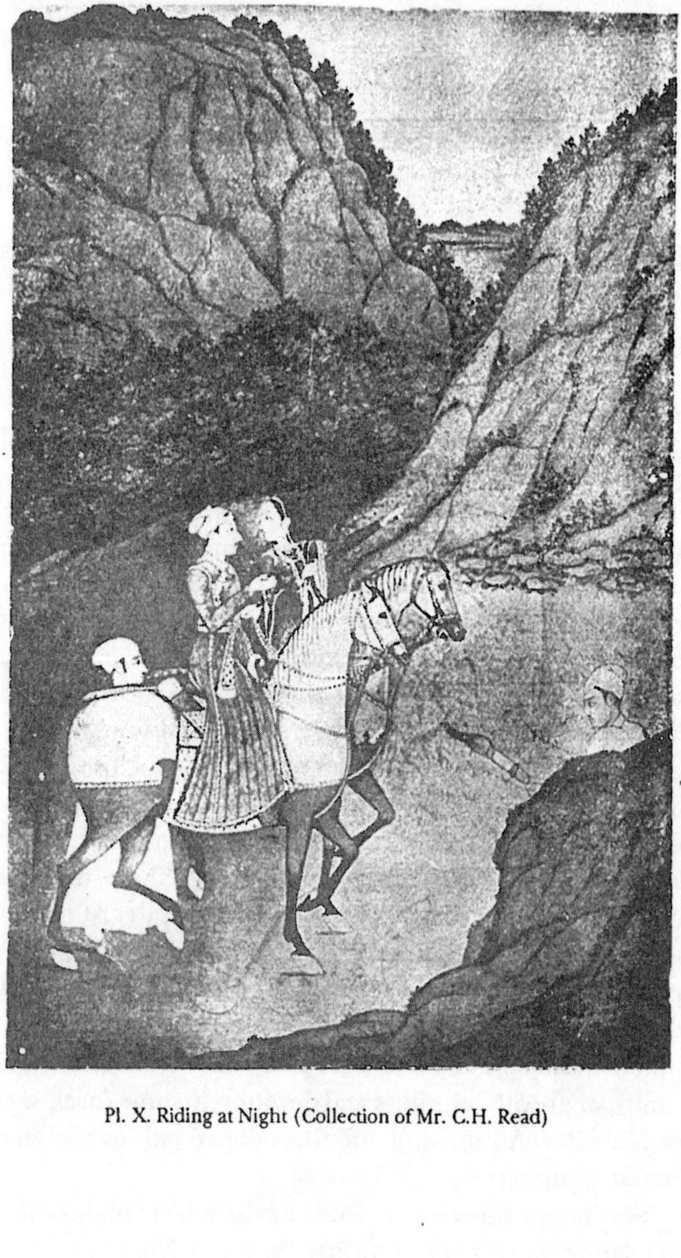

Pl. X. Riding at Night (Collection of Mr. C.H. Read)

Baz Bahadur and Rupmati (pl. X). Baz Bahadur ruled over Malwa, AD 1554-70. Rupmati was a Hindu poetess, famed throughout India for her beauty and learning. Their love is the theme of many songs. When Baz Bahadur, in 1570, was defeated by Akbar's General, Adham Khan, Rupmati took poison to escape him. The picture, or a variant of it in which the two are riding out by day to hawk, is represented in many collections. The example here given is one of two almost identical versions in the collection of Mr. C.H. Read.

Another picture (pl. XI) shows three Hindu girls two with fireworks, the third a servant, standing on a terrace, with a lake and low hills behind. The sweet serene faces and exquisite dresses, lit up by the 'golden rain,' stand out against the dark background of the night. Though not signed it is probably the work of the painter Muhammad Afzal, who flourished in the seventeenth century.

A third picture (pl. XII) represents a princess, attended by two maid servants worshipping at a forest shrine of Siva. In picture of this type the princess devotee is really Uma seeking by worship to recover the love of Siva given to her as Sati in a previous incarnation. The whole landscape speaks of Siva; the mountain side and the mysterious forest have a strange sense of consciousness. The central figure shines with the radiance which the painters of night effects knew so well how to suggest. These pictures recall the rendering of devotional concentration so characteristic of early Italian painting, with which their spiritual kinship is very near. Perhaps the latter owed much to oriental influences. It would be possible to illustrate many more examples of Indian night pictures, of subjects such as 'The Camp Fire,' 'Bhils Hunting,' 'Abhisharika'; one more must, however, suffice (pl. XIII). This, which has been called 'The Bride,' loses much in monochrome reproduction, especially as regards the pure gold overdress of the nearest figure. The picture is of most delicate and romantic loveliness and

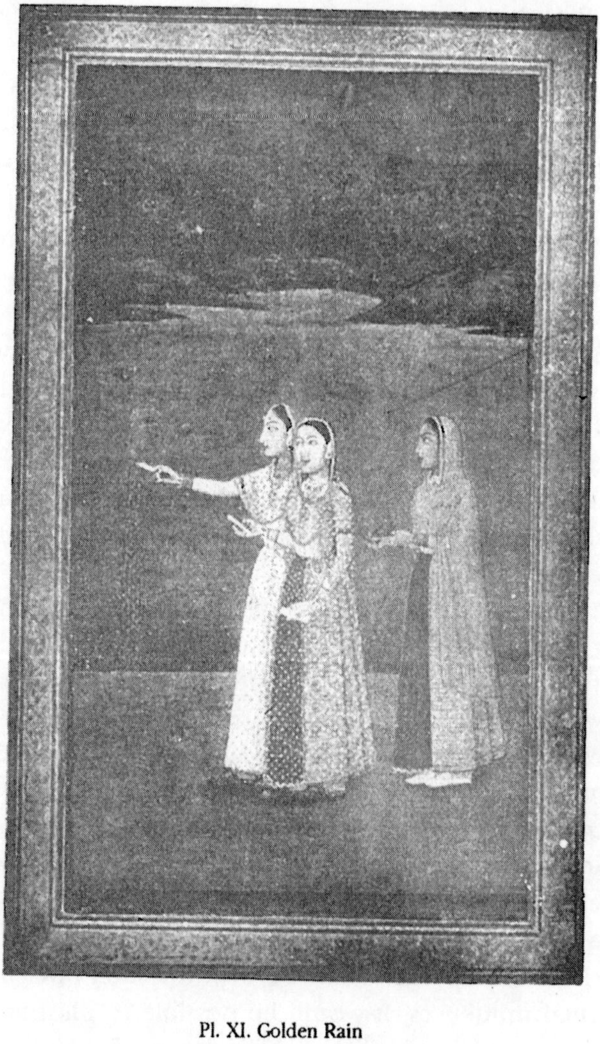

Pl. XI. Golden Rain

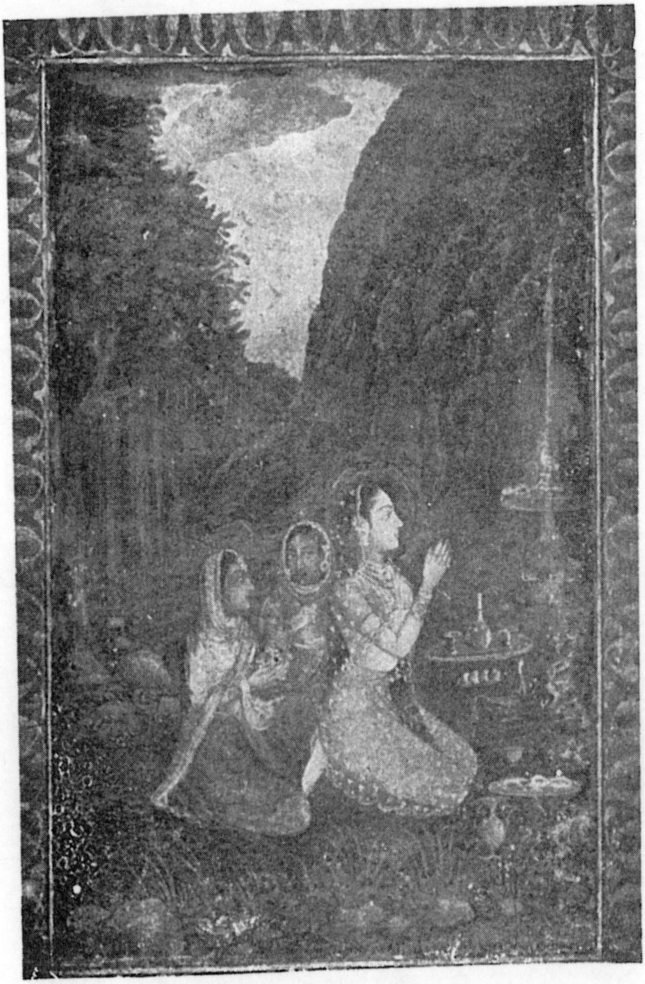

Pl. XII. Uma Worshipping Siva

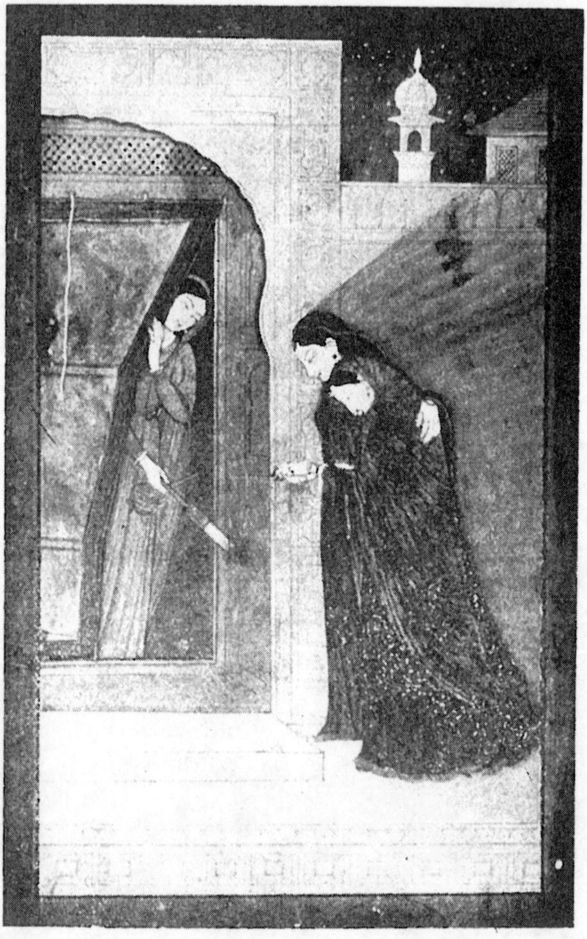

Pl. XIII. The Bride

purity. There is a haunting charm in the gentle shyness of the bride as she is led by a friend, perhaps an elder wife, to the bridal chamber. We may almost hear the wild beating of her heart and feel the tremulous touch of her red-stained fingers. A sleepy servant avails them with a torch and scent-spray. The light of the torch throws a deep shadow behind the advancing figures. The white marble buildings glisten in the moonlight. The whole picture bears the spell of that strange serenity and recollectedness, that so distinguish the old life of India, and survive so little in the life of non-rhythmic haste and hideousness into which it is so quickly changing. Perhaps it would not be possible to overvalue an art that brings to us so clear a message of calm and peace as do these romantic and religious Hindu pictures—a message from the time which we, taking an external view, sometimes think of as less peaceful and less civilized than our own.

# 10

## Song-Words of a Panjabi Singer

It sometimes happens that those who listen to Indian singers care more for the words than for the *ragas* to which they are sung, they have this excuse, that the words are almost always beautiful, while the singer's voice is sometimes harsh or inexpressive.

The words of Indian songs are almost exclusively lyrical, never markedly dramatic. They are often deeply passionate; never sentimental like the modern drawing-room songs of Europe. They recall rather mediaeval English and Elizabethan hymns and lyrics. Their burden of love or sadness is expressed in many poignant similes. They contain allusions to every phase and moment of Indian life. They make frank and simple use of physical symbols to adumbrate the deepest spiritual experiences. A vein of mysticism runs through nearly all.

There is no marked distinction between art and folk songs. The same musician sings words that are written in purely country speech, as well as in several literary languages, though if he be a hereditary minstrel or court bard he will probably apologise for the former, and himself prefer high-sounding language and elaborate musical variations. As a musician indeed, rather than a poet, though he is usually both, he often cares most for 'alap,' that is vocalisation, or songs without words, and naturally looks down upon those who prefer any words to pure music. The words of any art-songs however have a folk-character, inasmuch as their composers' names are by no means always mentioned, and indeed usually unknown, and inasmuch as the words of these songs are orally transmitted and may be collected in varying versions. It must always be impossible to draw any hard and fast line between folk and art songs, especially in a country like India, where the greatest works of literature have been for so long orally transmitted, and the musical notes of a song cannot be completely recorded and are rarely even partially written down. The adoption of musical notation, and extended use of writing and printing for the song words will certainly effect future changes in the character of Indian music, and lead to a more marked divergence of character in folk and art music, as has been the case in Europe.

Broadly speaking we may say at present as regards words, those are of the folk whose motifs are naive, whose rhythm is well-marked, where repetitions and refrains are characteristic, the language simple, and the number of verses not very small. As regards music, the folk songs are often sung to quite definite tunes which are not classical *ragas*. Their rhythm is emphasized. When sung to a *raga*, this has a set-form not admitting of *ad libitum* variation.

In art-songs the language and motifs are more or less literary, the songs are short, often rather impressions or suggestions than of a descriptive character. The comparatively few words are sung with continual repetition to classical *ragas* in forms admitting of almost unlimited variation. On the whole one may say that the art-singer treats his words with less respect than the folk-singer. In folk-songs also words and tune are inseparable: the art-singer will often sing any words to any *raga*, occasionally sometimes quite unsuitable. An interesting feature in the songs of northern India, to which I mainly refer, is the way in which they illustrate the fusion or mixture of Hindus and Moslem elements in the existing culture. This is well seen in the song-words translated here, which are selected from the songs of an *Ustad* of Kapurthala in the Panjab: they form only a fraction of his entire repertory.

A few words about this singer, in many respects a typical Panjabi musician of the present day, though on the whole much above the average, must be recorded before the actual songs are quoted. His name is Abdul Rahim, a hereditary 'Kalant,' now a pensioner at Kapurthala. His father, Aliyas, was formerly employed at Jodhpur. Abdul Rahim has a profound knowledge of classical *ragas,* and a sweet but not very strong voice, which he frequently overstrains, with expressive but often too violent gesticulation. His ancestors were Brahmans, forcibly converted in the time of Aurangzeb. Like so many other Panjabi Mussulmans, the family retain many Hindu customs especially in connection with marriage, e.g., non-remarriage of widows. His faith in the Hindu gods is as strong as his belief in Islam. He is both devout, and also what is nowadays called superstitious. He would, for instance, hesitate or refuse to sing Dipak *raga,* unless in cold weather, for fear of creating actual flame. He is somewhat 'foresighted' and has prophetic dreams, and is like his father, something of a Fakir. Slight and delicate, gentle-mannered, patient, a first-rate teacher, an inveterate smoker of hookah, a great boaster, somewhat over-fond of presents, learned in his own art, and at times truly inspired, yet finding that art now less appreciated than in the times of his predecessors—such are the salient characteristics of a rather pathetic figure, not without nobility, but such as the board school education of Indian universities finds little use for.

Turning now to the songs themselves, one finds that they belong to many languages—Panjabi (various dialects), Urdu, Hindi (various dialects, including Brij Basha), Sindi, Persian, Arabic. Those in Panjabi have naturally the most definite folk-character. This is most marked in the well known and delightful 'Lachchi,' of which only a few verses are here translated. The air in this case is also purely folk and is not a *raga.* Another and more poetical folk-song is sung to Pahari (mountain) *raga* and has for its refrain 'They sell in the market'. A third, rather in Dogri than Panjabi, is sung to Jog (separation) *raga*. Perhaps the most beautiful, because of its perfection and directness is the three-line love song, sung to a very exquisite form of Pahari, Chamba Pahari. The windy freshness and, so to say, the solidity and noble gravity of the tune here rightly fit the passionate simplicity of the words. Like nearly all Indian love songs, it is a song of separation, a lament for loneliness. The references to Jammu and Kashmir perhaps need the explnation that the Kashmir court winters in Jammu and spends the summer in Srinagar.

'Death', a beautiful lament for the beloved, expresses also the attachment of Panjabi people to their own land: in its third line, with pathetic hopelessness a woman prays her lord to return from the land of death, as if he had but gone away form home to another part of India or perhaps emigrated in search of work. Another little song, 'What means separation,' is purely impressionist, telling even less of a story than the last, and is appropriately sung to one of the most beautiful of midnight *ragas*.

In two songs reference is made to well-known romances. One is a Sufi quatrain, sung to Bihag or Malkaus in which reference is made to the Sindhi story of Punun and the other is taken from the Panjabi story of Hir and Ranjha. Hir tells her companions that by intensity of loving only, can union with the Beloved be attained: to forget love, even for a moment, is in itself separation.

The Panjabi *ghazal,* sung to Asa *raga,* is again a song of separation or loneliness, with a Sufi interpretation: and the curious little song 'Only four days' seems to lament the shortness of life—too short for anything but play.

Of Hindu songs the first quoted likens true love to that of a tree that itself bears the heat but shades others and also by a subtle metaphor of the kite and the kite-flyer suggests that love itself may be the cause of separation between Lover and Beloved (in the perfection of Love these are one and there is no room for 'loving' and 'being loved'). The magnificent futility of the last couplet—as if Love could fail to bring with it pain, or as if to proclaim that none should love would deter any from loving!—would be hard to surpass. A second Urdu song, expresses the ecstatic indifference of the Sufi to the voice of any but the beloved: its refrain '*koi kuch bolo,*' may be rendered '*aiunt, quid aiunt' aiant*!

A curious quatrain sung to Brindabani Sarang proclaims at once the singer's faith and mentions his favourite airs. It is a mixture of Musulman and Hindu ideas.

The invocation sung in Darbari Kandra, is an example of the prayers addressed to Moslem saints, usually asking for material blessings.

Passing now to the Hindi songs, we find many about Krishna, sung by this Musulman with as much devotion as if he himself were a Vaishnava. The first praises the one Lord appearing in many forms, proclaiming the unit of Brahma, Siva and Vishnu, though speaking most of the latter in His incarnations as Krishna, Rama and Narasimha. Three other songs are Gopis' complaints, and refer to the boyhood of Krishna at Brindaban.

One curious couplet asks 'What yogi is this?' Another complains 'You never speak to me now.' These are distinctly art songs, sung with constant repetition of words and phrases to complicated *ragas*.

'How can I soften the heart of my Lover,' literally *kapata ki ganth*, 'the knot in the heart,' is again a lament for loneliness or separation: the phrase calls up the classic words of the *Mundaka Upanishad*.

'Of him who sees that which is the highest and the lowest—*the knot of the heart (hridaya-granthih) breaks*—all his doubts are solved—and his works become nothing.'

Thus in the words of Indian, as of Sufi songs, the human and divine are made one.

Much less beautiful than any of these, but yet characteristic, and much admired by minstrels, are the fulsome panegyrics sung to reigning kings by Court bards of the past. These are often sung to quite unsuitable *ragas*—as if one should set words even more extravagant than those of 'See the conquering here' to an air by Corelli or on the air of a mediaeval carol. In both the songs of praise quoted, the rulers hymned are hailed, with questionable taste and to modern ears, a suggestion of irreverence, as more than gods.

The few songs' quoted form, as remarked, only a small part of one singer's repertory. If we except the two last, we cannot fail to admit their beauty and variety: and in India there are still thousands of singers possessed of a similar store. Would that some would collect, publish and translate some of these treasures! They will not always be at our disposal. For to the educated (as the victims of our Universities, Missionary and Nationalist colleges are by grim irony called) they are unknown and often meaningless. A well educated Indian professional man once asked me 'what is a Sufi?' On another occasion a well-known Nationalist enquired 'what is a Gopi?' Little use to think of an 'Indian people,' when such are the fruits of 'Indian' education!

## 'LACHCHI': FROM THE PANJABI*

Aha, where Lachchi spills water,
Spills water, spills water, spills water,
There sandal grows—where Lachchi spills water.
Aha, Lachchi asks the girls
The girls, the girls, the girls,

*I have to thank my friend Dr. Piara Mall for assistance with most of these translations, especially those from the Panjabi.

Oh what coloured veil suits a fair complexion?
Aha, the girls said truly,
Said truly, said truly, said truly,
A veil that is black, becomes a fair complexion.

What then your fortune Lachchi?
Your fortune Lachchi, your fortune Lachchi, your fortune Lachchi?
Lo! Your boy like the moon, what then your fortune?

Who'll give you milk to drink Lachchi?
Drink Lachchi, drink Lachchi, drink Lachchi?
Your friendship with the goat-herds is sundered!
Who'll give you milk to drink?

### 'BAZAR VAKENDIAN', RAGA PAHARI: FROM THE PANJABI

Thou who knowest my inmost self, Beloved,
Who knowest myself,
—They sell parched grain in the market—
If thou camest to my house, then would I tell thee my sorrow and joy,
My Beloved, who knowest my self.

Thou bowl of my dowry,
Thou bowl of my dowry
I sent thee away at midday, but now I wish I had not—
My Beloved, who knowest my self.

Thou veil of my dowry,
Veil of my dowry,
I earn but dishonour because of my friendship for thee,
My Beloved, who knowest my self.

On the high roof when I churn the butter,
  When I churn the butter,
My parents rebuke me, thou alone can'st console—
  My Beloved, who knowest my self.

They sell good spindles and fine in the market,
  They sell in the market
The eyes of thee too are bewitching,
  My Beloved, who knowest my self.

Aniseed they sell in the market,
  Aniseed they sell,
May Miranji cross-roads ever be populous, where first we had speech,
  My Beloved, who knowest my self.

They sell curds in the market,
  Curds in the market,
Thou shalt sit near no wanton, lest they name thee a rake,
  My Beloved, who knowest my self.

### 'RAJA OF THE HILLS', RAGA JOG: FROM THE DOGRI

Come sometimes to our land, Oh Raja of the hills, come sometimes to our land!

God made your country prosperous,: were I
  A cloud, I would pour down on my beloved's land:
Come sometimes to our land!

### 'JASMINE', RAGA CHAMBA PAHARI: FROM THE PANJABI

Jasmine is blooming in my courtyard, and malthi gives scent near my bed:

O beloved, thy service was in jasmine but perforce must thou go to Kashmir

I send letters, but get not one in reply, to tell of thy welfare!

## 'DEATH': FROM THE PANJABI

My Lord has not spoken, he sulks since the afternoon—
The wheat crops are ripe, the rose trees in bloom—
I need not thy earnings, only come to the Panjab again!
You are setting out on your journey, but I am left desolate,
Ah, the house and the empty court do fill me with fear.

## 'THE HEART OF PUNUN', RAGA BIHAG OR MALKAUS: FROM THE PANJABI

There is separation's melting flame in the heart of Punun, who daily lights its sacred fire:
The fire of disunion giveth no peace, as straw stays not its flame.
He himself is fire and fire-maker, he himself burns, and causes to burn.
How then can Hashm peacefully sleep, who has drunk of Love's cup?

## 'WHAT MEANS SEPARATION?', RAGA BIHAG: FROM THE PANJABI

I know not, dear one, how separation, from thee befell;
What is separation, he knows, who after meeting his parted,
I know not how it may be!

## 'PANJABI GHAZAL': ASA RAGA

Draw aside thy veil, O Beloved, that I may see thy face, who seek thy glance,
To see thy face for one moment I would sacrifice a hundred moons on face,

All my comrades wish than lovers he or than bads.
I, luckless one, remain alone crying and crying and sighing.
Some come full, some go filled, the turn of some comes (and why not mine?)
Some desiring water swim in tanks, some called from their homes lie bosom to bosom:
I, luckless one, am nothing whatever if in the heart of my Lord I am forgotten.

## 'ONLY FOUR DAYS', ASA RAGA: FROM THE PANJABI

Only four days to play, Oh mother, only four to play!
To play and play!
Night has fallen, my Beloved is far from me, mother.
See, mother, thou woulds't have me spin—but four times I bend the spindle,
Four, Oh mother, four only to play.

## 'HOW HIR WON RANJHA?' FROM THE PANJABI

The Sakhis are asking thee, lovelorn Hir, by what merit you won Ranjha
'I left my spinning, I left my carding, Love indwelt in each pore of my body,—
By this merit, O sakhis, I won Ranjha:
When my lovelorn soul one moment forgot, that night Ranjha came not.

## 'RAGA MIAN KI BHAIRAVI': FROM THE URDU

They are fools who set their love on what does not seek for it:
No heart has the candle, in whose flame the moth burns to death.
Love thou in such wise as a tree—

Bearing the heat of the sun on its head and giving to
others shade.
Beloved, think not that disunion from thee brings peace!
The wet forest wood smoulders day and night.
Beloved, in those days when thou wert the kite and I the
string,
The wind of Love blowing made separation between us.
Beloved, had I known that Love would bring pain,
I must have proclaimed with beat of drum that none
should love!

## URDU GHAZAL*: ASA RAGA

I am mad for my Beloved:
They say, what say they?
Let them say what they will!
Take me for a fool or a mad man:
They say, what say they?
Let them say what they will!
I have nothing to do with them,
Whether they be pleased with me or angry,
May One only be gracious to me!
They say, what say they? Let them say what they will!
The Shaikh walks around his holystead;
I offer up myself at thy altar,
Call it shrine or hovel.
They say, what say they? Let them say what they will?
I have gazed on the glory and sheen of the cheeks
of my Beloved,
I am burnt up as a moth in the flame,
I am as one drunken:
They say, what say they? Let them say what they will!

*See Also *Eassys in National Idealism*, ch. XIII.

## 'MY FAITH AND MY RAGAS', RAGA BRINDABANI SARANG: FROM THE URDU

Thou Allah! art all, who showed forth the model, so has knowledge come to the prophets:
My clan is Sayyid, my tribe is Moulah, my faith is in God and His prophet Muhammad.
My first is Bhairon, my second Malkaus, my third Handol, my fourth Siri Raga.
My fifth is Megh, my sixth is Dipak, thus Sujan has sung.

## 'INVOCATION OF A SAINT', RAGA DARBARI KANDRA: FROM URDU

Hazrat Ghaunzal Samdani, Kutab of Rab, Oh Mir, come thou, who hast lordship over all sultans!
Friend of god, Abdulqadar Jailani, make easy what is hard, give us bodily health, thou hast Allah's favour on thee!

## 'PRAISE OF THE LORD', RAGA NEKI KANDRA: FROM THE HINDI

Thou as Krishna appearedst, as Rama, Lakshman without stain Thyself took form!
Thyself, Mahadev, art a shining beam, Thyself art Brahma who established the Vedas.
Thyself the three Vedas, Thyself the three worlds, Thyself the Tapas, Thyself the Yogi who Yoga established,
Thyself became fish of the sea, Thyself took the form of Narasimha!

## 'GOPIS' COMPLAINT', RAGA BIHAG: FROM THE HINDI

See, sakhis, how Krishna stands!

How can I go to fetch water, my mother-in-law?
When I go to draw water from Jamna!
There meets me the young boy of Nand!

## 'GOPIS' COMPLAINT', RAGA MALKAUS: FROM THE HINDI

When I go down to draw water, O mother, at Jamna ghat,
He catches me by the clothes and twists my hand:
When I go to sell milk,
At every step Gokula seeks to stop me.
When he is so obstinate what can I say?
He ever comes and goes: why does this Youngling so?
He takes hold of my arm and shuts my mouth, and clasps me close:
I will make my complaint to Kans Raja, then I shall have no fear of thee!

## 'WHAT YOGI?', RAGA BIHAG: FROM THE HINDI

What yogi is this, who wanders about with rings in his ears and ashes smeared?
Some perform meditation, some dwell in the woods, some call on thy name with devotion!

## 'YOU DO NOT SPEAK TO ME', RAGA DARBARI KANDRA: FROM THE HINDI

You say nothing to me, though Phagan has come
Every watch you are sulky with me, always I see you with others.

## 'HOW CAN I SOFTEN THE HEART OF MY LOVER?' RAGA LACHARI: FROM THE HINDI

How can I loosen the knot that binds the heart of my beloved?

All my sakhis well-decked have gone to their lovers,
But I sit alone eating poison.

## PRAISE OF RAJA RAM OF GWALIOR: FROM THE HINDI

Raja Ram, Raja of Rajas, Maharaj, Adhiraj, accomplished,
 Treasury of ten kinds of knowledge!
Whosoever asks his wish is heard and reward obtained:
 do homage to Him who established the Vedas, Raja Ram!
Eight Siddhis, nine Nidhis dost thou bestow,
And gifts to the wisdom-endowed!
Tan Sen gives praise. He who worships the Lord will
 freedom win, may Raja Ram live through four ages!
(By Tansen)

## PRAISE OF RAJARAM OF JODHPUR RAGA BHOPALI: FROM THE HINDI

Sun of India! Ras Raj! at the splendour of whose might
 even Rama trembles,
The seven islands, nine spheres, and four continents
 have done homage to thee, the powers of the air take
 refuge in thee,
O glory of the Lunar dynasty, they praise thee in fear,
 thou the ruler of Jodhpur!
(By Fakir Aliyas, father of Abdul Rahim)

# 11

## Poems of Rabindranath Tagore

*'Man has no body distinct from his soul'* (Blake). It would be difficult to exaggerate the significance for Indian nationalism, of such heroic figures as that of Rabindranath Tagore, the Bengali poet, dramatist and musical composer: 'for nations are destroyed or flourish in proportion as their poetry, painting, and music are destroyed or flourish'.

The work of Rabindranath is essentially Indian in sentiment and form. It is at the same time modern. The literary revival in Bengal, like the similar movement in Ireland, is national, and therefore creative: it is a reaction from the barren eclecticism of the universities. This reaction is voiced, not by those who ignore or despise, but by those who have most fully understood and assimilated foreign influences. For it is not deep acquaintance with European culture, that denationalises men in Asia, but an imperfect and servile apprehension of it. Those who understand the culture of others find in it a stimulus not to imitation but to creation. Those who do not understand become intellectual parasites.

The pure politician is often no nationalist at all, in an idealistic sense. The kingdom of Heaven is within: so also is the freedom of nations. The Pole adhering to his language and traditions, preserving in himself something of character and individuality, is more free despite his fetters, than Indians would be tomorrow if every foreigner left their shores for ever. It is the work of poets (poet, painter, sculptor, musician, 'artist,'—all these are synonyms) to make their hearers free: it is they alone who establish the status of nations.

The present age is peculiarly indifferent to poetry: peculiarly lacking in that sense of wonder which alone enables us to understand them. To the few that are with us, and who serve us in spite of ourselves, we owe more than common love: and the time has come now for response. Those love the poets who do their will and whom their singing moves.

One of Rabindranath's poems is about a sannyasi who passed his life in seeking the touchstone, and was so intent on the search that at last he passed it by unknowingly.

## THE TOUCHSTONE

A wandering madman was seeking the touchstone,
With matted locks, tawny and dust-laden, and body
shrivelled and worn to a shadow,
His lips tight-pressed, like the shut-up-doors of his heart,
His burning eyes like the lamp of a glow-worm seeking
its mate,
(One cannot but smile at the thought that this hearthless
and homeless vagabond
With only a rag to cover his nakedness, owning kinship
with none in the world,
Should despise gold and silver and make light of king's
treasures,
Should hunger for no other thing than the touchstone.)
Before him the endless ocean roared: wave after wave
Rose and laughed at the madman's persistent delusion,
The sky with lidless eye gazed at him, the wind rushed
about him,
Day after day the sun climbed up from the sea and the
moon appeared in the evening.
The garrulous waves ceaselessly talked of hidden treasures,
Mocking the ignorance that knew not their meaning:
Men came and men went on the shore, some laughed
and some wept,

Still the madman roamed in search of the touchstone.
May be he now had no hope remaining,
Yet he rested not, for the search had become a part of his life—
Just as a bird whose mate has died
Calls to her all night long in vain—
Just as the ocean for ever lifts its arms to the sky for the unattainable—
Just as the stars pursue their course, seeking a goal that can never be reached—
Even so on the lonely shore, the madman with dusty tawny locks
Still roamed in search of the touchstone.
One day a village boy came up and asked
'Tell me, O Sadhu, whence and what is this golden chain about your waist?'
The Sadhu started—the chain that once was iron was verily gold;
It was not a dream, but he knew not when it had changed.
He struck his forehead wildly—where, O! where had success been attained unknowingly?
It had grown into a habit, to pick up pebbles and touch the chain,
And to throw them away without looking to see if a change had resulted:
Thus the madman unwittingly found and lost the touchstone.
The sun was sinking low in the west, the sky was of gold,
The sea like molten metal, the western Lady dreaming golden dreams:
The sannyasi returned on his footsteps to seek anew the lost treasure,
But his strength was gone, his body bent, and his heart in the dust, like the torn bough of a tree.

The old unending path lay lifeless before him.
The desert sand gleamed in the dusk, the night grew
grey:
So the madman began again his search for the treasure
For which already one half of his life had been spent.

The painters of our visions—the makers of our songs—the builders of our houses—the weavers of our garments, these all are a touchstone that can turn to gold for us both past and present, if we will it so. These, if we would let them, could lead us back to a world we have lost, the world to which our real greatness belongs, a world for which nothing can ever compensate. There is more hope for us than for the weary madman: for we have poets as our guides to take us back to the elemental and real things in life. They can show to us the significance of little things, the wonder of what is always going on. They tell us that we are what we are not because of knowledge or wealth or power, but because of the dolls in our childhood's games, because of the rivers that we worship as divinities, because of the skill of craftsmen and the loneliness of saints, because of the beauty of women, and the splendid indifference of men to danger and to death.

There have been two great phases of religious thought in India which we may call Saiva and Vaishnava, using these terms, however, in an unsectarian sense. The impact of modern science has brought into prominence the more severe, intellectual and philosophical or Saivite phase: for the philosophy of the absolute stands unshakeable alike by the old superstitions of priests and the new superstitions of science. This religious philosophy is the intellectual charter of those who hear the call of the Infinite, the logic of renunciation. It is Siva who brings not peace, but a sword, and Kali is the destroyer of time: 'he that will lose his life for my sake shall save it, but that will save his life shall lose it.'

Contrasted with this philosophy is the humanism of Vaishnava thought. Even in the *Bhagavadgita,* based as it is upon the Upanishads, there is a continual endeavour to place the philosophy of action without attachment on the same level with the philosophy of inaction and denial. In more definitely Vaishnava literature there is a constant glorification of life, a delight in sensuous symbolism, a consecration of humanity, that is foreign to the sterner philosophy of Shankaracharya. Vaishnava art is correspondingly humanistic, and it is from this school of thought that the poetry of Rabindranath Tagore derives. In it are echoed the teaching of such pophets as Sri Chaitanya, and poets such as Jayadev and Chandidas, who sang of the Religion of Love. Life itself is not an illusion, but an ever present manifestation of God. This is the burden of 'Renunciation' and the 'Way of Salvation'.

### RENUNCIATION

At midnight the would-be ascetic announced:
'This is the time to give up my home and to seek for God,
Ah, who has held me so long in delusion here?'
God whispered 'I,' but the ears of the man were stopped.
With a baby asleep at her breast lay his wife
Peacefully sleeping at one end of the bed:
The man said 'Who are ye that have fooled me so long?'
God said again 'It is I,' but he heard not the voice—
The baby cried out in its dream, nestling close to its
  mother—
God commanded 'Stop, fool, leave not thy home',
But still he heard not. God sighed and complained
'Why does my servant wander to seek me, forsaking me?'

### THE WAY OF SALVATION

Not my way of Salvation, to surrender the world!
Rather for me the taste of Infinite Freedom

While yet I am bound by a thousand bonds to the wheel.
This cup of the Earth will ever be filled for me
With thy nectar of varied colour and fragrance, O God;
From thy lamp in a thousand flames I will light
All my world and illumine Thy temple divine.
Not my way the repression of senses or searching within
me by yoga!
In each glory of sound and sight and smell
I shall find Thy Infinite joy and bliss abiding:
My passion shall burn as the flame of salvation,
The flower of my love shall become the ripe fruit of
devotion.

## THE METAPHYSICS OF A POET

Let any who will, ponder with eyelids closed,
Whether the Universe be real, or after all an illusion:
I meanwhile sit and gaze with insatiate eyes.
On the Universe shining with the light of Reality.

## SALVATION

Closing my eyes and ears, withdrawing my mind and
thought,
Turning my face away from the world,
Shall my little soul all alone cross over
This awful sea to gain salvation at last?
Beside me will sail the great ship of the Universe
The cheerful canoe of voyagers filling the air
With spreading sails gleaming white in the sun—
Her freight of human hearts, how beautiful!
Far on and on she will sail
With laughter and tears through alternate darkness and
light:
Through Infinite space will echo sadly

The sound of their joys and sorrows.
When all the Universe sails away with this cry
What avails it for me to seek salvation alone?

An older, and in some respects a deeper, certainly a sadder note is struck on other poems such as 'Janmokatha' (the story of Birth), and 'Biday' (Farewell) and 'The Guide'. In these, the insistent sense of impermanence alike in life and in self carries us back to the Buddha's vehement denial of 'soul' and his consolation of the mother who would not be comforted—'Foı which Jiva do you sorrow?' He asked.

THE GUIDE

I asked of Destiny: 'Tell me
Who with relentless hand pushes me on?'
Destiny told me to look behind. I turned, and behold
My own self behind pushing forward the self in front

JANMOKATHA

'Where have I come from, oh where did'st thou find me?'
A baby is asking its mother:
Folding the babe to her breast,
Half crying, half laughing, she answers—
Thou wast the desire of my heart,
My dearest darling!'

'Thou wast in the dolls of my childhood's games,
And when I made figures of Siva in clay,
I made and unmade thee then:
Thou wast enthroned
With our household god:
In his worship, I worshipped thee,
My dearest darling!'

'In all sweet hopes that ever were mine
In all my loves and desires
For the life of my mother and in grandmother's life
hast thou lived.

In the lap of the Lady
Who rules in our house
Thou hast for ages been hidden,
My dearest darling!'

'When in girlhood my heart
Like a flower was opening,
Thou wast a sweet fragrance about it:
Thy own tender softness
Thou gavest, unknown,
To my youthful form,
My dearest darling!'

'Thou pet of all shining ones,
Thou eternal, unchanging,
Co-aged with dawn—
From the world's dream-life
Thou wast borne on a torrent of bliss
As a real thing to play with my heart,
My dearest darling!'

'As I gaze on thy face
Thy mystery I cannot understand:
Thou belongest to all and how can'st thou be mine!
My body I kiss in thine
Since now thou art mother's babe:
Laughing thou cam'st to the world,
My dearest darling!'

'Lest I should lose thee
I hold thee tight to my breast
I cry if I see thee not every moment!

I know not what snare of maya
Could entrap the world's treasure
In these slender arms of mine,
My dearest darling!'

## BIDAY
### (Farewell)

Mother darling, let me go, oh! let me go!
In the dim and early dawn,
When you stretch your empty arms
And cry 'Oh, Baby mine!'
I shall whisper 'Baby is not here'—
Mother darling, let me go.

I shall be but a breath of the blowing wind
And pass by your breast as a sigh—
You can never hold me fast in your arms.
I'll be a wave of the water
And none can ever know what I am,
When you bathe, I shall play all around you.

When at night the rain falls down in showers
You will lie in our bed alone and think of me;
The patter of drops on the leaves will be my voice,
I shall flash in lightning through your windows
Do you think you will know my wild laughter then?
Mother darling let me go
When the night is late and dark
And you are wakeful and sad
I'll be a star and softly whisper 'Sleep, mother dear!'
When at last you are sleeping, worn and tired,
I'll be the moonbeam that rests on your bed,—
And kiss your sweet closed eyes.

If your eyelids are open ever so little.

I shall come peeping in as a dream,
  And love you while you're asleep;
Then you will wake with a start,
  And feel for me in the bed—
But I shall have vanished, where nobody knows.

  In the Puja holiday time
Children will come to play in our garden;
  They will say that Baby is not in the house—
But even then in the sound of the flute
  I shall pass through the sunlit sky,
And follow you in all your work in the house.

  When aunty comes and questions you
  —With holiday gifts in her hands—
  'Sister, where has your Baby gone?'
Say to her, 'Baby is everywhere,'
  He is in the pupils of my eyes,
He is on my breast and rests in my lap!

  Mother darling, let me go, oh! let me go!
In the dim and early dawn,
  When you stretch your empty arms
And cry, 'Oh Baby mine!'
  I shall whisper 'Baby is not here'—
Mother darling, let me go!

The Buddhist pantheism (to use a paradoxical phrase) of these songs closely links Indian with Japanese conceptions of race and individuality. In another way it reminds us of such western pantheism as that of Oscar Wilde. There is much, too, suggestive of poetry that belongs to what is known as the Celtic revival: it is not strange that the thought of the two Indians, one in Europe and one in Asia should approach for all national movements throughout the world are the stirring of one spirit.

Through all Rabindranath's songs there runs an undertone of sadness: this must always be so in the work of serious men. This sadness is not gloom, but rather a secret joy, that perceives with unfaltering vision the splendid pageant of life, but looks upon death as an adventure awaiting no less glorious achievement. One of the sweetest of the small lyrics, a four-line song to Death might be a gentle, more feminine echo of Whitman's magnificent 'Joy, Shipmate, Joy,' just as the 'Metaphysics of a Poet' recalls his 'Terrible Doubt of Appearances.'

### DEATH

O Death, had'st thou been but emptiness,
  In a moment the world would have faded away.
Thou art Beauty: the world like a child,
  Rests on thy bosom for ever and ever.

### THE CREATION OF WOMEN

O woman, you are not merely the handiwork of god,
  But also of men; these are ever endowing you with
    beauty from their hearts.
Poets are weaving for you a web with threads of golden
    imagery,
  Painters are giving your form ever new immortality.
The sea gives its pearls, the mines their gold, the summer gardens their wealth of flowers
To deck you, to cover you, to make you more precious:
The desire of men's hearts has shed its glory over
    your youth.
You are one-half of woman and one-half a dream.

### IS IT TRUE?

  Tell me if this is all true, my lover,
Tell me if it is true.
  When the eyes of me flash their lightning on you

Dark clouds in your breast make stormy answer:
Is it then true
That the dew drops fall from the eyes of night when I
am seen,
And the morning light is glad when it wraps my
body round?
Is it true, it is true, that your love
Travelled alone through ages and worlds in search
of me?
That when you found me at last, your age-long desire
Found utter peace in my gentle speech and my eyes
and lips and flowing hair?
Is it then true
That the mystery of the Infinite is written on this
little brow of mine?
Tell me, my lover, if all this is true?

Rabindranath Tagore's father, Maharshi Devendranath Tagore was a leader of the Brahmo Samaj movement in Calcutta, a man of great personal piety and deeply religious. He was the heir to great wealth, all of which he renounced to satisfy the claims of his father's creditors, though not legally bound to do so. He sought always for the Infinite and universal. Rabindranath inherited his father's enthusiastic nature. Of a very sensitive aesthetic and mystical temperament, his nature reached to every fine emotion whether in life or art or religion.

Out of the materials of these emotions he has, to use his own metaphor, woven for his country a web of golden imagery glorifying and recreating Her loveliness. Mysticism, the sense of the Unity of life, is for him inseparable from the delight in all sensuous beauty: he is Vaishnava and Vedantist is one, believing, like Blake, that man has no body distinct from his soul, and the five senses are the chief inlets of soul in this age.

Two main influences affected Rabindranath in boyhood, that of his father, and that of Vaishnava poetry. He accompanied his father on his widely extended travels to the Himalayas, and in the plains and by the rivers of Bengal. At fourteen he produced a sort of musical opera, called 'The Genius of Valmiki'. At seventeen he was sent to England, and studied at University College, London, for a year. He visited England a second time without any intention of studying, his relations by this time despaired of his worldly prospects.

Returning to India, Rabindranath became almost a recluse. He lived for long periods in a boat on the Padma, the main stream of Ganga, in the Nuddea district of Bengal. The profound influence of this lovely river scenery which was for so long familiar to him is again and again reflected in his poems and prose stories.

It was not till Rabindranath reached middle age—about forty—that this long period of growth bore fruit. Since then he has poured fourth a veritable stream of poems, stories, plays and other works, the key-note of which is the sense of the manifestation of god in the daily and elemental realities of life. His work, however, is not merely literary: he founded at Bolpur, in the west of Bengal, a school over which he still presides. In this quiet ashrama, where classes are held out of doors under the mango trees, Rabindranath brings to bear upon successive generations of adoring students the influence of his great personality. He thus exercises both a direct and an indirect influence upon the development of modern Bengali life and art.

The translations convey only a shadow of the original poetry, they give only the meaning, that in the songs themselves is inseparable from their music. Some are based on versions supplied to me by Mr. A.K. Chakravarti, others on translations given to me by the author himself. Some of them may perhaps convey a hint of the delicate charm of the originals and the perfect unity of thought with emotion that is expressed in them; but those who would really know them, must understand their language—best of all if they hear the poet himself recite them.

# 12

## The Modern School of Indian Painting

In the nineteenth century the traditions of Mughal and Rajput painting may be said to have finally disappeared, largely as the result of the change of taste produced by "English Education" so called. A certain amount of work in oil-painting and water-colour was practised as the result of School of Art Education. The late Raja Ravi Varma was the best known of these painters in a purely European style, but neither he nor any other workers of the pseudo-European school attained to excellence. His work at the best reached a very second-rate standard. Nevertheless, Ravi Varma's work is but too well known and widely distributed in India through the medium of cheap oleographs, which do not even give it a fair chance. Inferior even to the work of Ravi Varma, is that of some other painters in Bombay and Madras.

The work of the modern school of Indian painters in Calcutta is a phase of the national re-awakening. Whereas the ambition of the nineteenth century reformers had been to make India like England, that of the later workers has been to bring back or to create a state of society in which the ideals expressed and implied in Indian culture shall be more nearly realised.

The co-operation of two differently gifted men made possible a great change in the public attitude towards art. Mr. Abanindronath Tagore, an Indian painter already of great promise, encouraged by Mr. Havell, then Principal of the Calcutta School of Art, began to seek inspiration in the seventeenth century Hindu and Mughal paintings, which had, till then, been so little appreciated. At the same time

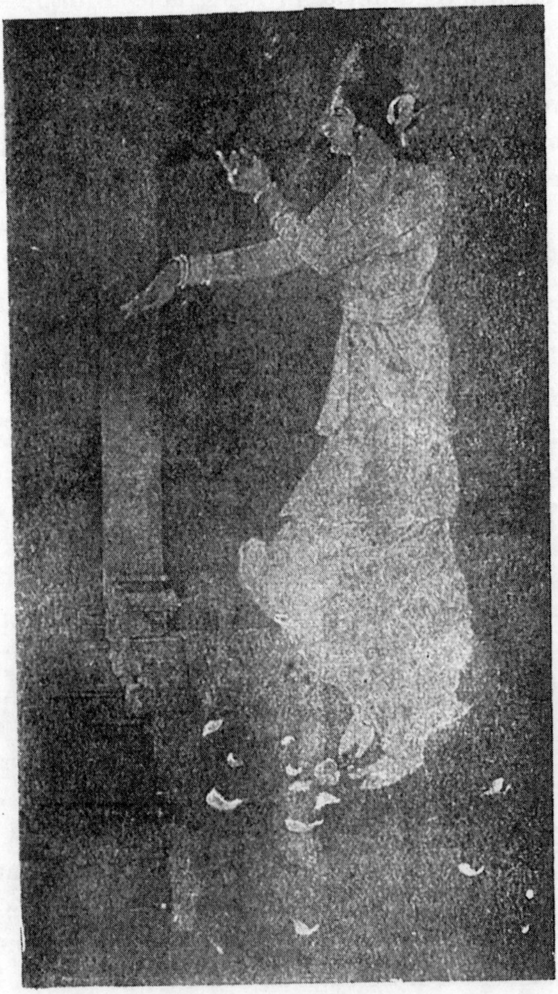

Pl. XIV. Devadasi (by A. N. Tagore)

Mr. Havell was fortunate in being able to dispose of the collection of inferior European paintings which belonged to the School of Art, and to replace them with fine examples of seventeenth century Indian work. The collection thus begun is now one of the most important of its kind. It is remarkable evidence of the former state of feeling that this move was not effected without strenuous opposition on the part of students and the Nationalist Press, so strong was the belief that Europe must be the only source of artistic inspiration. Those days have long gone by.

Mr. Abanindronath Tagore (now Vice-Principal of the School of Art) has been the teacher and leader of a small school of painters in Calcutta, whose inspiration and technique have been as far as possible Indian. Mr. Tagore has painted many pictures himself, and has designed frescoes for the new School of Art building. His pupil, Nand Lal Bose, has already produced much important work. Surendranath Ganguly produced some important pictures, but has unfortunately died. Ishwari Prasad is a descendant of hereditary painters at Patna, and is a teacher in the School of Art. Mr. Gogonendronath Tagore, brother of the painter, has developed a gift for drawing portraits and landscapes in monochrome in a very delightful and clever way. Venkata Appa, a student from Mysore, has produced work of real promise. Asit Kumar Haldar, Hakim M. Khan, and Samarendranath Gupta, are the best known of the younger students. These painters have received much assistance from the members of the Indian Society of Oriental Art formed a few years ago in Calcutta, for the study of Indian art in all branches, and the encouragement of the modern school of Indian painters. This society has held more than one exhibition of old and modern work—especially at Allahabad in 1910-11—which have done much to win for both the recognition they deserve.

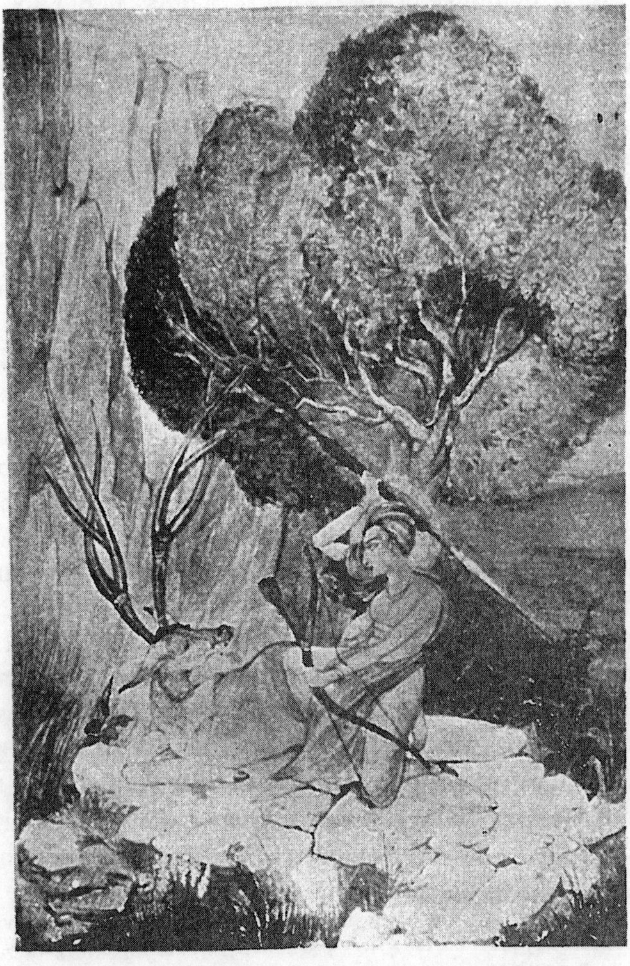

Pl. XV. Rama and the Magic Deer (by A.N. Tagore)

Several paintings of the Calcutta school, mostly by Mr. Tagore himself, have been reproduced in the *Studio*, *Modern Review*, and in Mr. E.B. Havell's *Indian Sculpture and Painting*. The *Studio* has published a series of Mr. Tagore's illustrations of the *Rubaiyat of Omar Khayyam*.

The subjects chosen by the Calcutta painters are taken from Indian history, romance and epic, and from the mythology and religious literature and legends as well as from the life of the people around them. Their significance lies in their distinctive Indianness. They are however, by no means free from European and Japanese influence. The work is full of refinement and subtlety in colour, and shows a real love for all things Indian; but contrasted with the Ajanta and Mughal and Rajput paintings which have in part inspired it, it is frequently markedly lacking in strength.

The paintings of the Calcutta school have been lavishly praised, and severely criticised both in India and in England. This at least shows that they are of some significance. In England the severest criticism has come not from old-fashioned and narrow-minded or academic critics, but from such writers as Mr. Roger Fry, whose appreciation of classic Oriental art, whether of India or the Far East, is very real.* Mr. Fry writes "Such pictures as that of the 'Siddhas of the Upper Air' show that, however anxiously these artists strive to adopt the formulae of their ancestors, the spirit that comes

*"What", asks Mr. Fry, "will be the effect upon Western art of the amazing revelations of these last twenty years? One can scarcely doubt that it will be almost wholly good. When once the cultivated public has grown accustomed to the restraint, the economy of means, the exquisite perfection of quality, of the masterpieces of Eastern art, it will, one may hope, refuse to have anything more to say to the vast mass of modern Western painting. And then, perhaps, our artists will develop a new conscience, will throw over all the cumbrous machinery of merely curious representation, and will seek to portray only the essential elements of things. In thus purifying pictorial art, in freeing it from all that has not immediately expressive power, Western artists will be merely returning to their own long forgotten tradition. The greatest practical value of Eastern art for us lies in the fact that those essential principles which, in our thirst for verisimilitude, we have overlaid, have been upheld with far greater constancy by the artists of the East."

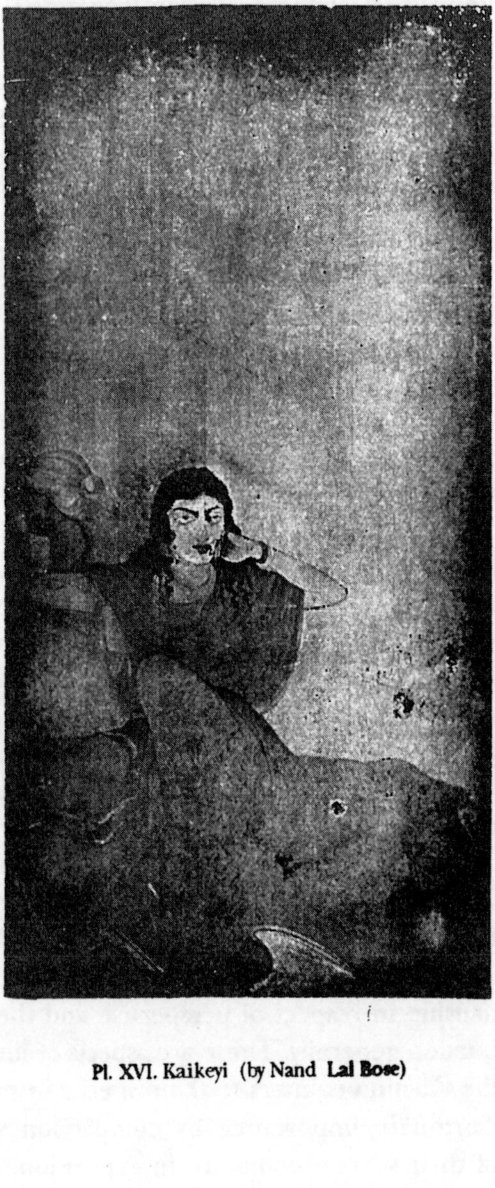

Pl. XVI. Kaikeyi (by Nand Lal Bose)

to expression is that of the American magazine illustrator. Nothing, indeed, could provide a stronger proof of the profound corruption which contact with European ideas has created in Oriental taste than these well-intentioned but regrettable drawings." This criticism, so far as it goes, is fairly justified. Most of the Calcutta paintings are graceful; but they are often sentimental in conception, weak in drawing, and *tamasic* in colouring. This especially applies to the mythological and heroic subjects. None can portray the gods but those who have themselves seen them; to modern India, the gods are shadowy and unreal. They are too barbaric, too irrelevant, for the belief of minds enlightened by the wisdom of the West: and though to the Calcutta painters themselves, their own belief seems real, their work inevitably reveals the extent to which they are affected by the modern attitude. They have been anxious to make beautiful pictures, rather than moved by sheer necessity to self-expression. Again, the colouring of many of the Calcutta pictures, especially the later, Japan-influenced, work of Mr. Tagore, is muddy in the extreme, and the tones throughout so low as often to make the very subject of the picture hard to decipher. This is as far as possible a departure from the pure clean colour schemes of earlier Indian art, although its vagueness lends charm to the treatment of certain subjects. Turning now to Indian writers, we shall find that the criticism there applied to the work of the Calcutta school is practically negligible, since it has been confined to unessential matters such as deficiencies of draughtsmanship in respect of perspective and the science of representation generally. These are aspects of illustration in which the Calcutta painters took no special interest, and are of subordinate importance by comparison with the question of their success or failure in expression.

So much for unsympathetic criticism. It may be conceded that there is essential truth in what has been thus said. But

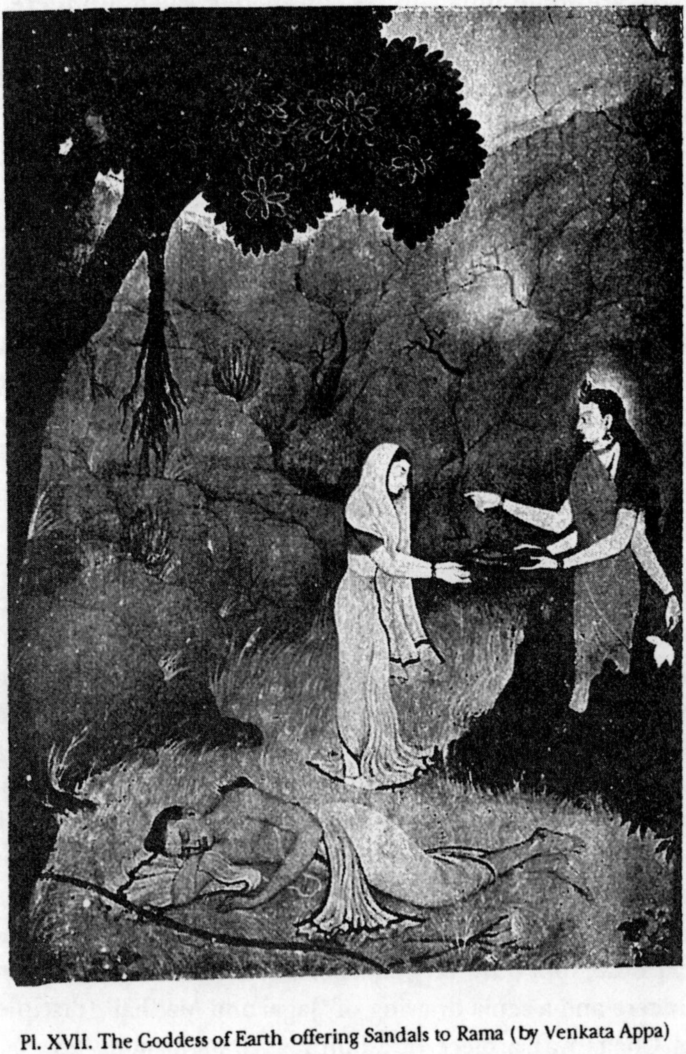

Pl. XVII. The Goddess of Earth offering Sandals to Rama (by Venkata Appa)

there are some things to be considered which are therein overlooked. In the first place, whatever else it may or may not signify, at least the work of the Calcutta painters and its partial acceptance in India, marks a revolution in taste, a reaction from the absolute banality and vulgarity of the formerly admired works. Those who are familiar with the nature of the influence of European upon Indian art during nineteenth century, and the squalid, uninspiring and wholly foreign character of Indian education, making Indians strangers in their own country, can only wonder at the possibility of even so much reaction as has taken place during the last ten years. Nor can those fairly judge the work of the Calcutta school, who do not make themselves personally acquainted with its *ateliers,* and all the young enthusiasm which is there spent in serious effort to find some effective means of escape from a state of aesthetic stagnation far worse than the Early Victorian, with which the English Pre-Raphaelites had to deal. Again, amongst the actual paintings produced, there are some of real achievement and high promise. The earlier work (e.g., the illustrations to the life of Krishna) of Mr. Tagore himself is full of movement and colour; Mr. Venkata Appa's 'Earth goddess offering sandals to Rama, pl. XVII', and 'Sankaracharya and the Toddy man' are really beautiful and naively expressive, and Asit Kumar's larger paintings of Krishna as a baby (pl. XVIII) are straightforward and unaffected, and their colour pure. Some works by Nand Lal Bose, too, have very excellent qualities: his 'Sati' is very sincere and a sepia drawing of 'Jagai and Madhai' (disciples of Chaitanya) a piece of admirable draughtsmanship.

Moreover, these painters care only for Indian subject matter and sentiment, and this is an essential preliminary for any true revival of Indian painting or sculpture, since no art which is insincere, can ever be great. The whole Calcutta movement has also done much to secure protection and

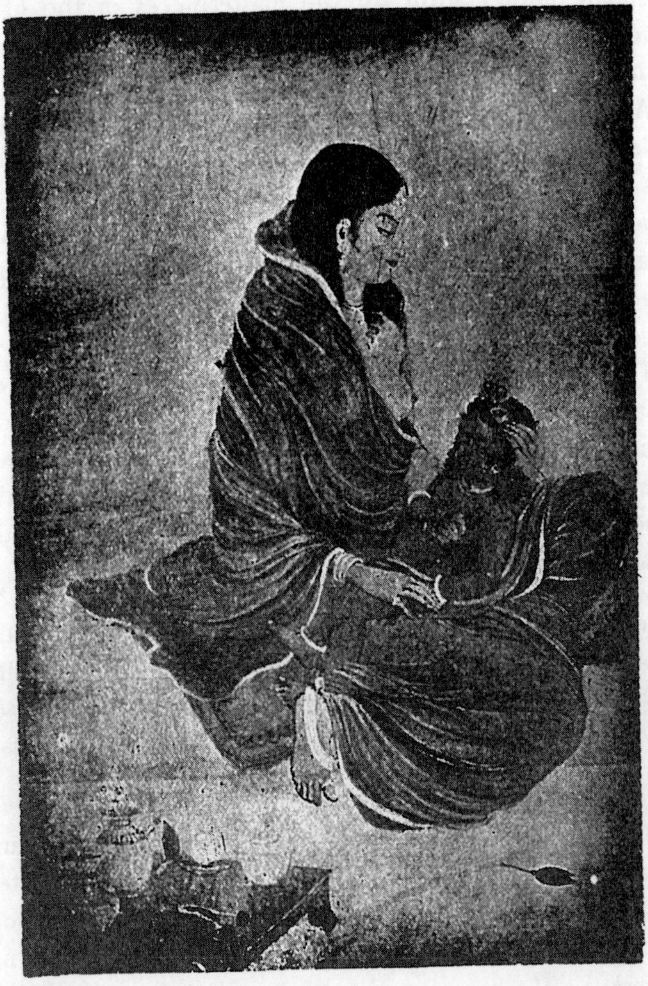

Pl. X. Riding at Night (Collection of Mr. C.H. Read)

adequate appreciation for the masterpieces of the older schools, and some of its members have done excellent work in making copies of the frescoes at Ajanta.

A great responsibility now rests upon the members of the Calcutta group, *and upon the public* for whom they work. What has been accomplished constitutes, considering the very adverse conditions obtaining in India a few years ago, and to almost the same extent at the present day, much; but it is not one half or a quarter of what the world has a right to expect from India.

The East, however, at the very moment when its real greatness is becoming apparent to the West, is losing its hold upon its own treasure. A recent writer in the *Athenaeum* already clearly perceives this tendency. Admitting the superiority of Eastern to Western art in the past, he finds the reason for it in the fact that,

> In the East men have ever set the emotional above the practical life, and the artists have excelled in expressing the very essence of material things because they expressed what they felt, instead of representing what the ordinary man sees.

But the present is no time for complacency on this account; for the pendulum is swinging the other way. The same writer, speaking of the "vulgarity of sentiment, flashiness of execution, and ape-like imitation" in much modern Japanese painting, remarks,

> Few observant people will deny that there are signs of an awakening in Europe. The times are great with the birth of some new thing. A spiritual renaissance may be at hand. Meanwhile, Japan is 'forging ahead.' Already she has set her hand to the task of civilizing, that is to say, Europeanising China just at the moment when Europe is coming to

loathe her own grossness. Time is the master of paradox. Who shall say what surprises are too fantastic for his contriving? Can the classic distinction between East and West be after all mutable? Is the unchanging East changeable?... London may yet be the spiritual capital of the world, while Asia—rich in all that gold can buy and guns can give... glorious in all material glories. . . postures, complacent and obtuse, before a Europe content in the possession of all that matters.

This at least is taking place in India, and movements like that of the Calcutta artists, are as yet too local, and too little intensely passionate to suffice to hold back the destroying tendencies. All the more on this account we ought to expect and demand much from them; for the principal lack in modern Indian art is due to the non-existence of an educated public wanting or understanding art at all—not to the lack of artists. The "English-educated" Indian public wants only to be amused and interested, while the political section wants only to possess and does not think of giving.

# 13

## Education in Ceylon*

The most pressing problem which awaits our consideration in Ceylon at the present time, is the general question of education,—educational problems and racial idealism. Idealism, seriousness, and almost an extreme spirituality have been, in the main, characteristic of oriental civilisations in past times. Especially in India and Ceylon we have behind us a very great tradition, as I think, the greatest tradition which men have anywhere inherited. To be more precise, we have the knowledge of past supreme greatness in religious philosophy, in literature, in art and in commerce. We do not now excel in any of those things. If we omitted the lawyers for whom formerly there was no use in Ceylon, we should be hard put to it at the present day to find amongst our communities men deserving of very high honour amongst us. In other words, we have developed during the last century in the direction of intellectual parasitism. We have, during that period, created nothing, although we may have assimilated much. And if history has for use any lesson, it is that in the ultimate judgement which is passed upon nations in the course of time, nations are judged by what they have created and not by what they have assimilated or by their prosperity, commercial and financial, considered at any given period. Now, I want you to consider with me on the one hand our past greatness—and when I say "our" I speak of course,

*Extract from Dr. Coomaraswamy's speech as Chairman, Annual Ceylon Dinner, December, 1911.

of India and Ceylon as one country—and of the steps we should take to make it possible to fulfil our duty to that past greatness in the future. The revolutions of time are indeed, amazing. It is no longer in the East, but in Europe, beneath the surface of international politics and commerce, that the most idealistic movements are carried on at the present day. Everywhere, on a greater or less scale one observes that idealistic experiments are being made and idealistic propaganda being put forward in Europe and America. Nor is the Western World unaware of what is happening. To quote the words of a recent writer in *The Athenaeum* it is only too apparent that "London may yet be the spiritual capital of the world, while Asia, rich in all that gold can buy, and guns can give, glorious in all material glories—postures, complacent and obtuse, before a Europe content in the possession of all that matters." I think it is a little saddening for us Orientals to feel that such a criticism of our modern life is only too well founded.

To review the idealistic movements and tendencies in modern European culture, would require a series of lectures. I need only refer briefly to the many schemes for the improved organisation of Society which are put forward from the most impossible Utopias to the already realised Garden Cities and town plannings, to the revival of separate national cultures all over Europe with their protest against the premature destruction of national character and their accompanying phenomena of creative art, as in the case of the Irish drama and their accompanying rediscovery of existing poetry as in the case of English folk songs; to modern humanitarianism with its ramifications in the direction of animal protection and prison reform, to the arts and crafts movement in England, and its correlatives on the Continent and in America, and above all to the new education of which the foundations were laid by men like Froebel and Pestalozzi and the traditions of which are being carried on by workers like Professor Geddes and Professor Sadler and Mr. Hudson at the present day, in this country and by many others abroad.

I must also refer to a movement to which I give the name in my own mind of "The Discovery of Asia". The far-reaching character of Asiatic influence on Europe at the present day is scarcely realised and I think it will not be realised until we are able to look back in perspective on what has happened. Nothing of the same kind has ever taken place before. It is true, of course, that early Mediterranean civilisation was essentially of an Asiatic character. It is also true, as Professor Lethaby so eloquently tells us, that the flowering of mediaeval art in Europe was the result of a previous "long filtration of the Oriental spirit to the point of saturation;" but with the Renaissance the receptivity of Europe came to an end, and Asia, though in a sense more familiar, came to be regarded only as a country to be exploited. To this end, also, the scientific materialism of the middle and latter part of the nineteenth century, which was the logical outcome of the Reformation, largely contributed by its depreciation of the imagination, and its consequent disvaluation of our religious ideals and the general basis of our social structure in the East. In this depreciation, I fear that we have too tamely acquiesced. But now all these things have changed with bewildering rapidity. Western science is no longer a study of mechanism, but has become philosophical and, if I mistake not, there has been and is still going on in Europe, a religious revolution which has made it far more possible than for many centuries it has been, for Eastern and Western minds to understand each other's modes of thought. I refer specially to the widespread modern interest in mysticism as a human phenomenon which cannot be ignored, a variety of human experience which cannot be overlooked. There is in fact, a growing sense of Unity as the fundamental basis of all religious experience, whatever its local forms and ritual. I think this wider outlook on the part of the Western nations, their new appreciation of the ideas which have so long been current in Asia, have made it possible for the two sides of the world to meet one another in a more friendly way than used to be the case. This has gone hand in hand with the appreciation of Oriental philosophies due to the work of such men as Deussen and Schopenhauer, and interpreters such as Sister Nivedita, Pierre Loti, Fielding Hall and Lafcardio Hearn which was opened to the Western world a new conception of Eastern life and thought, and a new conception of the wonderful seriousness and beauty of our social and family life and of the degree of education which Oriental women have achieved—a point which I think more than any other Western nations have misunderstood, and which perhaps has made it difficult for them to appreciate our civilisation, as they are now beginning to do. Lastly we have the newer but very serious interest in Oriental art which is being taken in Europe. It began with Japan and has now extended to Persia and India and of this I may remind you that an interesting example is afforded by the recent foundation of the India Society, in which English and Indians and other Continental ladies and gentlemen combined for the study of the aesthetic aspects of Indian culture. We find before us not only an enormous amount of work to be undertaken but many willing workers to undertake it, and I think that work of this kind does more than anything else to bring together people of different countries because we have a common object which overrides all personal considerations. Even the existence of Oriental music is now admitted. *The Discovery of Asia, then, has become to Europe no longer a piratical expedition, but a spiritual adventure.*

We have remarked that our national genius is no longer creative, but now, I ask you, leaving that question aside, whether we have taken any part in these European idealistic movements of which I have spoken, whether indeed in Ceylon we are even aware of them. I ask you also whether we have played any part in bringing our treasures to the light of others, whether in fact, we have assisted at all in this Discovery of Asia of which I have spoken? I think that on the contrary we have allowed to fall into decay and disrepute all those elements in our culture which constitute its greatness, and we have acquired in exchange only a too superficial veneer of that Western civilisation which is in Ceylon doled out to us in the name of English education, a name for which I have too much respect to think that that which goes by it in Ceylon has any right to do so.

A predominating factor among the various causes of our present intellectual poverty alike in India and Ceylon, I find in the limitations of the educational systems obtaining. From an educational system at once secular and so unreal, I do not think that anything else but intellectual poverty could result. When I say secular, I do not mean that our education in Ceylon is not definitely Hindu or Buddhist or Christian. I mean that it does not stir our imagination or awaken in us any sense of wonder. In particular this limitation is conspicuous in connection with the present methods of teaching physical science, divorced from philosophy, binding the mind in a superstition of facts more difficult to escape from than any superstition of the fancy by which we may have been enthralled in the past. When again I call our education unreal, I mean that it is not related to our experience and the ideals which we already accept. It does not make us wish to do better than we have done already but teaches us that all we have done is foolishness. "If you find yourself," said Ruskin, in a noble passage which I will quote to you "set in a position of authority and are entrusted to determine modes of education, ascertain first what the people you would teach have been in the habit of doing, and encourage them to do that better. Set no other excellence before their eyes, disturb none of their reverence for the past, do not think yourselves bound to dispel their ignorance, or to contradict their superstitions; teach them only gentleness and truth; redeem them by example from habits which you know to be unhealthy and degrading; but cherish above all things local associations and hereditary skill."

Now gentlemen, what is there in the education which is given us today in Ceylon which cherishes local association and hereditary skill? I am sure that none of you could point to anything. I need not tell you in fact, that modern education in Ceylon does the opposite of this. It does so from the time, when in the infant school, children are taught to spell out "Johnnie picked the apple", without having any conception of what an apple tree may be to the time when our young ladies who are working for the Cambridge Locals are taught as a finishing accomplishment, a little French or, as I have heard in one case, what was asked for by the parents as "a few strokes on the violin" before she left.

I believe that the greatest work before us in India and Ceylon, a work which may well occupy all our energies for half a century is that of reforming and reconstructing our education.

Now, I do not refer here to elementary education, but rather to secondary education, for though elementary education is necessary and must be more widely spread than is the case at present, I do not understand the position of those who think that it is more important that everyone should learn to read or write than that the work of master-minds should sway the hearts of men. I do not think that universal Board School education in India and Ceylon will do for the illiterate peasants what the works of Valmiki and Tulsidas and Kamban and Manikka Vacagar have already indirectly or directly done for them throughout that great

Continent. The education of the Indian peasant and the Indian woman is already admirable. It is indeed a limited education, but very few of us are, or are likely for a long time to be, qualified to improve it. It is idle to think that the three R.'s in themselves will restore to modern life that reverence for learning and sensitiveness to beauty which it has lost. What we need is the education of leaders and that education of leaders means the education of ourselves, for that responsibility is upon those of us who have received the most complete and fullest education, and especially those of us who go into other parts of the world to learn what we may learn there and bring it back for the benefit of our country. What we need then is the education of leaders. I think that the illiterate are in some ways better off than we, for they have only to learn, but for too many of us, we have a great deal to unlearn.

I have spoken so far generally both of India and Ceylon, but now I shall refer only to Ceylon in making practical suggestions for our country in the future. I think our first necessity is a Local University.

I say this not only for the many excellent reasons which have already been put forward by other members of the Ceylon University Association, but also because I think that no education is inspiring except where research and discovery are going forward and the spirit of wonder is felt. I think that in this university the predominating control should be given to Ceylonese, not because at present they are any better qualified than Englishmen to determine modes of education, but because responsibility will make them bound in honour to qualify themselves. Education in Ceylon is not now too European. It should be more European in spirit and less European in form. The spirit of modern European education, even in England to some extent, is national. I should like to see deputations of Ceylonese young men sent to Europe, to

Denmark, France, Hungary, Finland, Ireland and also to America and Japan to study what is being done by leaders of education here, see what experiments are being made, and learn what education really means. I should like them also to study very seriously Indian history and culture for two years. Above, all I should like them to come under the personal influence of men like Professor Geddes and women like the late Sister Nivedita. They would then be qualified by knowledge and responsibility as they should be even now by inheritance, to shape and create. Now, let us suppose that such a Committee were in existence and try to formulate a few suggestions for their consideration. In the first place, let more money be spent on education, not more men, not more schools, but higher salaries for teachers, sufficient to secure the services of leaders, for men are of more consequence than curricula. Let them seek for these leaders in every part of the world in America, Europe, India and Japan, wherever they may be found, as well as in Ceylon, and give them power. Do not let them be, unless in exceptional cases, officials of any kind.

Now, the greatest necessities of the present time are the relation of education to the Ceylonese life of today, and the full recognition of our intellectual inheritance. We need to devote more attention to languages. I think most of you will agree that English history, language and literature, is most imperfectly taught in Ceylon. I would make of English a far more important a study than it is now. Even more neglected are the indigenous and most sweet languages of Ceylon, Sinhalese and Tamil, and all the corresponding culture that goes with them. Using the terms Ceylonese to cover both languages and cultures, I would make compulsory in every leaving examination and an essential preliminary to further professional or technical education an equally intimate knowledge of English and of Ceylonese. I would abolish the compulsory teaching of all other languages in Ceylon, particularly Greek and Latin. I do not think it is worth while to teach any language where there is no possibility of, say, half any class taught, proceeding far enough to take pleasure in reading its literature in the original. In saying this I do not refer to modern languages like French or German which may be taught for practical purposes, but I would not have the Greek language taught at all in Ceylon except exceptionally and individually. This is not because I think so little of Greek, but because I think so much of it, and because I think so much of life; a little Greek grammar as taught in the colonies does not spell educational life, but rather the reverse. May I remind you that the Professors of Greek language and literature and history at Oxford are themselves ardently in favour of the suppression of compulsory Greek in the University of Oxford and then you will realise that it is not necessary to be prejudiced against Greek culture and language to think it is not necessary for it to be taught in Ceylon. I do not know what those professors would think of our Greek, if they think the interests of Greek culture are not served by compulsory Greek in Oxford. Let me give you my own experience. I did a certain amount of Greek for the London Intermediate Arts and could translate any part of Sophocles' *Electra* a good many years ago. But I cannot now read, much less translate, three words of Greek which I may find in a quotation. I do not think my school Greek affected me at all, in fact, or that I owe anything to it. But a good many years afterwards I began to read translations from the Greek, being led thereto by interest, first romantic literature and afterwards, in religious philosophy and art. In that way I acquired some real interest and knowledge of the Greek spirit which a little Greek grammar never brought me. There is no need to despise translations, because there have always been from time to time men of a peculiar genius like Sir

Richard Burton, William Morris, Lady Gregory, Edward Fitzgerald, and Gilbert Murray, who in their chosen language, have been so admirably qualified to translate the spirit and beauty of the original into their Mother Tongue as to make it possible to understand the spirit of the foreign culture almost as well, and indeed far better than, one would do by an imperfect knowledge of the foreign language itself. Nothing but a most perfect knowledge of Greek, for instance, would enable any one to acquire a better knowledge of the Greek spirit than he could gain by reading Jowett's *Plato,* and Professor Gilbert Murray's translation. I do not think any educationist would quarrel with me in this.

I have a practical suggestion to make in connection with Ceylon and it is a sort of compromise which I hope may meet with the approval of those who are so strongly in favour, as some are, of the retention of the classical languages as a means of education in Ceylon. This compromise is that we should set up in our colleges for the benefit of those few who would now by studying Greek, not the Greek language as a subject, but the study of Greek culture. There should be prescribed such books as Butcher and Lang's *Homer,* Gilbert Murray's *Euripides* and *Greek Literature,* Jowett's *Plato,* Lowes Dickenson's *Greek View of Life,* Miss Harrison's *Prolegomena to Greek Religion* and some good books on Greek art. I think a serious study of the Greek culture carried out on that basis and with the improved study of English, which I propose should form part of our future education in Ceylon, would do far more to familiarise anyone with the fundamental basis of European culture than a little Greek Grammar or the attempt to translate unseen Greek on the part of a few students at the present day. That is a suggestion I make, not only with regard to a possible University in the future, but as an idea that may be worked out at the present time and which would form a common ground between the classicists and those who would abolish the teaching of the Greek language in Ceylon.

Now I come to the last and most important point of my argument for the reform of education in Ceylon, that our University must be above all a school of Oriental learning, sufficient not only for ourselves, but to attract scholars, from all parts of the world to learn the wisdom of the East in the East. The more I know of Ceylon the more inseparable from India does it appear, and indeed, I regret sometimes that Ceylon and India are not at present under one administration. It might have saved us from difficulties in our life which arise from our attention to the University of London and the Cambridge Local Examination, in which examination, let me say for the benefit of the few who are not familiar with the conditions in Ceylon, no provision whatever is made for the study of the language which is spoken in any of the homes in Ceylon, (with the exception of English which is spoken in a few). Further, the more I know of India, the more wonderful and beautiful appear to be her past achievements. If then we would attain the liberty of spirit which is the true end of education, if we would recover our lost character of Orientals, we must turn to India and base our education on Indian ideals. We have already proposed to do this to some extent when we provided for the study of Sinhalese and Tamil as compulsory elements in our education. I now propose to make a third compulsory subject of Indian Culture in the same sense as I spoke of Greek culture, (though the Greek culture would not be compulsory except on those who would now be taking the Greek language). It should be studied in translations and studied in historical and descriptive works: there is more than ample material for such study even without the learning of any of the Indian languages which would present the first considerable difficulty. I was not bred on Indian soil, yet now when I go about among my friends in

India, I often find that they quarrel with me because I am much too Indian in my ways of thinking for their reformed and Anglicised tastes; so that I can assure you that, given the will, you will not find it difficult to secure with the means already available, a serious appreciation of Indian culture. I should have then, in all our colleges, 'Professors of Indian',—not of any particular language, but men who by their enthusiasm and knowledge, would convey to us that understanding of the civilisation of that wonderful country which they themselves possess. Finally, for Degree and Post Graduate courses, we must restore to Sanskrit and Pali their place of honour as par excellence the classical languages.

Now, gentlemen, I do not believe that any one, however much attached to the status quo in Ceylon, he may be, would seriously deny that such an educational revolution as I have outlined would restore to us our national character, which ought to belong to us, and would make us better fitted to enter into and sympathise with the lives of our less literate countrymen in the villages on the one hand, and on the other to hold our own in any more distinguished and learned society where we may ourselves be called upon to take our place. As my last words, I pray you to set before your hearts as an ideal this Ceylon University, where East and West shall meet in one enthusiasm, the enthusiasm of those who learn because they want to know, and those who teach because they care so much for what they teach, that they can do nothing else. I ask you to think of that university with longing, because I believe that ardent wishes realise themselves more rapidly and mysteriously than we sometimes think.

# Index

Abdul Rahim 90-93
'Abhisarika' (painting) 82
Abul Fazl 70
Adham Khan, Akbar's General 82
Ajanta, painted chaityas at 63, 120, 125
Ajanta artists 63
Akbar 67, 68, 82
Aliyas (Fakir) 90, 101
*Arabian Nights* 25
*Athenaeum* 125, 129
Aurangzeb 70, 90

Babar 68
Baz Bahadur 82
Benares—brass 14; Kinkhab 14; Sari 6
be Bon, Gustave 52
*Bhagavadgita* 56, 106
'Bhils Hunting' (painting) 82
Binyon 69
Birdwood, Sir George 11, 12, 37
Blake 50, 102, 113
Bombay School of Art 41
Bose, J.C. 33
Bose, Nand Lal 118, 124
Botticelli 75, 76
Brahmanical art 49
Brahmo Samaj movement 113
'(The) Bride' (painting) 82
British Museum 69
Brown, Percy 40
Brussels carpets 9
Buddha 58
'Buddha, Ceylon' (statue) 57, 58
Buddhist—art 49, 69, 76; painting 72
*Buddhist Art in India* 51
Burns, Cecil 16, 36-42
Burton, Sir Richard 137
Butcher and Lang 137

Calcutta artists (*also as* painters) 127
Calcutta movement (in painting) 124
Calcutta, painters 121, 124; painting 121
Calcutta School (in painting) 116, 118, 121, 123, 125
Calcutta School of Art 11, 116, 118, 120
Cambridge Local Examination 138
'(The) Camp Fire' (painting) 82
Central Asian art 68
Ceylon University 139
Ceylon University Association 134
Chaitanya 106
Chakravarti, A.K. 116
Chandidas 106
Christ 24
Christian art 53
Cole, H.H. 34
Corelli 93
Curzon 11

Deussen 131
di Vinci, Leonardo 50, 60
Dickinson, Lowes 137
*Dimnah (Anwar Soheli)* 65
'Divine Cowherd' (Rajput picture from Kangra) 78

'Dying Man' (Mughal painting) 69

Eastern art 54
Eckhardt 56
*Electra* 136
Elizabethan hymns and lyrics 88
English art, history of 42
*Euripides* 138
European—architecture 12; art 2, 46; artists 2

Factory Commission 16
Fitzgerald, Edward 137
Foucher 51
Francia, Francesco 76
Froebel 129
Fry, Rogen 120, 122

Ganguly, Surendranath 118
garden of Eden 32
Geddes 130, 135
Giotto 76
'Goddess of Earth Offering Sandals to Rama' (paintings) 124
'Golden Rain' (painting) 84
Goldsmith's Hall, London 37
Golonbeff 69
Gothic art 49
Gozzoli, Benozzo 76
*Greek Literature* 137
Greek View of Life 137
Gregory, Lady 137
Grünwedel 45
Gupta, Samarendranath 118

Haldar, Asit Kumar 118, 124, 125
Hall, Fielding 131
Harrison, Miss 137
Havell, E.B. 3, 40, 116, 118
Hearn, Lafcardio 60, 131
Himalayan (or Pahari) Schools (of painting) 74
Hindu art 53, 70
Hindu chemistry, history of 35
Hindu—painting 73,116; sculpture 58
Holbein, portraits of 46
*Homer* 137
Hudson 130
Humanitarian League 26

Indian applied art 42-43
Indian architecture, modern 12
Indian art 5, 11, 36, 39, 42, 43, 48, 49, 53-55, 62, 63, 122, 124; preservation of 12; revival of 44; progress or decline of 45; English, French and German handbooks to 52
Indian artistic industries 12; tradition 12
Indian colouring and design 4
Indian Industrial art 11
Indian music, neglect of 4
Indian painting 37, 63, 72, 81; future development of 80; modern school of 116
Indian portfolio painting 64
Indian sculpture 56, 60
*Indian Sculpture and Painting* 120
Indian Society of Oriental Art 118
Indo-Persian painting 65, 68
Industrial Art of India 7, 15
Italian painting 65, 68

'Jagai and Madhai' (painting) 124
Jaipur school (of painting) 74, 75
Japanese painting, modern 126
Jayadev 106
Jehangir 65
*Journal of Indian Art* 1, 12
*Journal of the Society of Arts* 36
Jowett 137

Kabir 24
Kamban 133

Kangra drawings 74
Kangra School (of painting) 74, 75
Kelmscott Press 26
Kipling, Lockwood 12
'Krishna and Yasoda' (painting) 123

Lawrence, Sir W. 38
Lethaby 49, 130
London Intermediate Arts 136
Loti, Pierre 131

M. Khan, Hakim 118
Macmillan 11
Maindron 52
Manikka Vacagar 133
Mendelsohn 47
Middleton 49
Migeon 69
Mirzapur carpets 5
*Modern Review* 120
Morris, William 27, 42, 137
Mozart 47
Mughal—architecture 67, 68; art 65, 69; painting 67, 68, 70, 72, 79, 116, 120
Mughal Schools of painting 65
Muhammad Afzal (painter) 82
Muhammad Nadir of Samarqand (painter) 69
*Mundaka Upanishad* 92
Munro, Sir Thomas 43
Murray, Gilbert 137

National movement, weakness of (Indian) 3
National School of painting, Bengal 42

Oriental—art 55, 131; Music 131

Persian—art 64; painting 64
Pestalozzi 129
*Phaedus* 30
Plato 19, 23, 30
*Plato* 137
Pope, Professor G.U. 49
Prasad, Ishwari 118
Pre-Raphaelite Italian painting 76
*Prolegomena to Greek Religion* 137

Rajput painting 70, 73, 76, 116, 120
Rajput Schools, painters of the 68
Rajputana schools of painting 73,79
*Ramayana* 65, 74
Ravi Varma, Raja 116
Ray, Prof. P.C. 30, 34, 35
Read, C.H. 82, 83
Reformation 53, 130
Renaissance in Europe 41, 53,130
'Riding at Night' (painting) 81
Royal Academy, London 43
Royle 34
Rupmati 82
Ruskin 132

Sadler 130
Sankaracharya, philosophy of 106
'Sankaracharya and the Toddy Man' (painting) 124
'Sati' (painting) 124
Schopenhauer 131
Shah Jahan 65, 68
*Shah Namahs* 68
'Siddhas of the Upper Air' (painting) 120
Silpasastras 48
Sir Jamsetjee Jeejeebhoy School of Art, Bombay 36, 39
Sister Nivedita 131, 135
Siva, Tanjore (Statue) 58, 59
Smith, Vincent 51, 52, 69
Sophocles 136
South Kensington Museum 34
Spencer, Herbert 58
*Studio* 120
Sundaramurti Swami, Ceylon (Statue) 59, 61

*Suz-u-Gudaz* 65
Swadeshi—Companies 9; factories 6, 13; goods 5; literature 8; movement 7, 8; shop 1
Swadeshi imitations of European industrial art 14
Swadeshist politician 12

Tagore, Abanindra Nath 42, 117, 118, 120, 121, 124
Tagore, Gogonendronath 118
Tagore, Maharshi Devendranath 113-14
Tagore's Musical Opera: The Genius of Valmiki 114
Tagore, Rabindranath 102-3, 106, 112; his poems 103-13
Tamerlane, portraits of, in Bodleian, Oxford 69
Tansen 101
Theuth 30
*Tiruvachagam* 49
Tiruvalluvar 24
Tulsidas 133

United Provinces Exhibition 11
University College, London 114
University of London 138

Vaishnava—art 74; paintings 74; poetry 114
Valmiki 133
Venkata Appa 118, 123, 124
Victoria Memorial Building, Calcutta 41

Watt, Sir G. 13, 22
Whitman 112
Wilde, Oscar 111
Witt 34

*Yoga Vashishta* 65, 66, 68
'Yogis' (paintings) 65